WRITING
DEEP
SCENES

WRITER'S DIGEST
BOOKS

WritersDigest.*com*
Cincinnati, Ohio

For more resources for writers, visit www.writersdigest.com.

19 18 17 16 15 5 4 3 2 1

Distributed in Canada by Fraser Direct
100 Armstrong Avenue
Georgetown, Ontario, Canada L7G 5S4
Tel: (905) 877-4411

Distributed in the U.K. and Europe by F&W Media International
Brunel House, Newton Abbot, Devon, TQ12 4PU, England
Tel: (+44) 1626-323200, Fax: (+44) 1626-323319
E-mail: postmaster@davidandcharles.co.uk

Distributed in Australia by Capricorn Link
P.O. Box 704, Windsor, NSW 2756 Australia
Tel: (02) 4577-3555

ISBN-13: 978-1-59963-883-6

EDITED BY **RACHEL RANDALL**
DESIGNED BY **ALEXIS BROWN**
PRODUCTION COORDINATED BY **DEBBIE THOMAS**

DEDICATION

Martha

To my husband

Jordan

To Erik and Ben, always

ACKNOWLEDGMENTS

We are grateful to the forces that drew us together, particularly that sun-drenched first meeting by the water, suggested by our friend Susanne Lakin (and for several more inspiring meetings with like minds Nina Amir and Frances Caballo). We knew the moment we met that creativity was alive between us and good things would come into being. We also thank the writers who have taken part in our Writer Path retreats—your adventurous spirits helped us test and flesh out some of the material that went into this book. Of course, we are deeply grateful to Phil Sexton for his belief in our work, and to the most competent and gifted editor, Rachel Randall. Lastly, to our families, who stand by when our writer's minds are busy constructing new worlds.

ABOUT THE AUTHORS

MARTHA ALDERSON is known as the Plot Whisperer for her books on plot: *The Plot Whisperer: Secrets of Story Structure Any Writer Can Master*, *The Plot Whisperer Workbook: Step-by-Step Exercises to Help You Create Compelling Stories*, *The Plot Whisperer Book of Writing Prompts: Easy Exercises to Get You Writing*, and *Writing Blockbuster Plots*, and for the award-winning blog she manages, *The Plot Whisperer*, which has been awarded top honors by *Writer's Digest* from 2009 to 2015.

Martha has been exploring and writing about the Universal Story for the past twenty years as part of the plot support she offers to writers. More recently, she has expanded her work to include helping writers transform their creative lives.

She is currently filming two new video programs: *The 27-Step Tutorial: How Do I Plot a Novel, Memoir, Screenplay?* and *A Spiritual Guide for Writers: Secrets of Personal Transformation*.

She and Jordan co-lead Writer Path retreats: www.writerpath.com. Visit her website: marthaalderson.com

JORDAN ROSENFELD is the author of three novels, most recently *Women in Red*, and several writing guides, including *A Writer's Guide to Persistence*, *Make a Scene*, and *Write Free*. Her essays and articles have appeared in such publications as *AlterNet*, *Bustle*, *Creative Live*, *Family Fun*, *Mom.me*, *The New York Times*, *The Rumpus*, *Salon*, *San Francisco Chronicle*, *The Washington Post*, *The Weeklings*, *Writer's Digest*, and many more. Her book commentaries have appeared on *The California Report*, produced by NPR affiliate KQED radio. She created and hosted the literary radio program "Word by Word: Conversations with Writers" on KRCB, which won an NEA Chairman's grant in 2004. Visit her website: www.jordanrosenfeld.net.

TABLE OF CONTENTS

INTRODUCTION

Over the decades, in our work teaching plot and scene, we have come to see that writers are easily overwhelmed by the process of story making. *Where do I start? What happens next? How do I know which scenes go where? What does my character do now?* These are just a handful of the questions posed by the writers we've worked with. *Writing Deep Scenes* is designed to answer these questions (and many, many more) in two ways: at the scene level and at the plot level. In addition, this book also explains how plot and scene elements intertwine.

Writing Deep Scenes draws upon Martha's expertise in teaching plot (in her books in the Plot Whisperer series) and Jordan's expertise in teaching scenes (as evidenced in her book *Make a Scene*). It presents a multilayered, truly deep, and, we believe, *new* approach that explores the intersection of plot and scene, the most essential elements of the craft of writing. Scenes—in which you take characters on a moment-by-moment trek of transformation—are what make all stories vivid and memorable. But scenes must fit within a framework of meaning and tension so that your story doesn't run off the rails or get mired down. This is where plot design comes in.

You can either read this book from start to finish or pick the area you need to strengthen. We recommend you start with the first three chapters, which serve as refreshers on plot and scene, no matter your ultimate goal.

In chapter one, "Plot Overview," you'll learn about Energetic Markers, the essential, solid supports needed to build the base of your plot. In chapter two, "Scene Overview," we'll show you how to write strong, layered, and engaging scenes to create memorable, page-turning plots. We'll make sure you know exactly what a scene is, when you're in one, and the difference between scene and summary. In chapter three, "Scene

Types," we'll discuss the various kinds of scene types you can use to achieve different goals.

After the refresher chapters, *Writing Deep Scenes* scrutinizes both plot and scene at the micro level.

First, we discuss the three key "layers" at the root of plot and scene: *action, emotion,* and *theme.* Every strong story is dependent upon these layers. Simply put, action is what happens, emotion is how characters and readers feel throughout the journey, and theme is the meaning produced in the process.

Additionally, we'll show you how to explore the "shadow" and "light" sides of your characters' journeys—from less self-awareness to full awareness and emotional maturity—as they progress through their stories and through the stages of their emotional, spiritual, and/or physical integration. Shadow, as it pertains to the character, is best explained by Carl Gustav Jung, a Swiss psychiatrist and psychotherapist who founded analytical psychology. He defined shadow as an aspect of a character's personality to which she is oblivious. The shadow side of her includes everything outside the light of her consciousness, both positive and negative. As Jung explained: "Everyone carries a shadow, and the less it is embodied in the individual's conscious life, the blacker and denser it is." In deconstructing the plots and scenes of successful stories, we find the shadow side everywhere: in all action where the protagonist is not in control; in settings under the antagonist's rule; in turning points that twist the character into unfamiliar territory, forcing her to confront both her hidden flaws and skills; and in the imagery that describes these events. To the untrained eye, scenes appear to be unified and whole; by teasing apart the hidden layers, we shine a light on the shadow side—the subconscious, symbolic, and subtextual elements of stories—to reveal aspects writers can consciously integrate into their own scenes to create more exciting, dynamic plots.

Writing Deep Scenes will also teach you:

- how to recognize each layer of action, emotion, and theme individually, and how each contributes to the whole plot and plays at the scene level.
- how to create the three layers utilizing the concepts of shadow and light.
- how to create a scene-by-scene layout of a character's plot that integrates action, emotion, and theme.
- how to create an intricate relationship between the emotion in a plot and the action in a plot in every single scene.
- how thematic imagery embedded in scenes increases a story's tension and readability, and contributes to the story's meaning.

Throughout the book, we cite contemporary scene examples from a variety of genres and story presentations, offer scene types to use at each crucial plot juncture, and provide methods for creating page-turning tension by layering in symbols and imagery. Where scene types are repeated, the information about those scenes expands to include nuances not addressed in previous chapters.

When you finish this book, you will be able to look at your own fiction with a deeper gaze, and you will possess a layered and integrated understanding of how to plot at the scene level.

Let's get started.

THE BASICS

CHAPTER ONE

PLOT OVERVIEW

Think of plot design as a musical act and scenes as the many, varied notes and tones a writer can choose from to compose a layered, riveting story. Once you learn to identify the fixed Energetic Markers—the key junctures that appear, universally, in all great stories—and to play with types of scenes to create appropriate drama and nuance at the buildup to and location of the Markers, your story will transform into one that readers can't put down. In this chapter, we'll discuss the basics of plotting and the information you'll need to carry with you as you read this book.

DEFINING PLOT

In all stories, to one degree or another, plot is how the dramatic events (action) in a story change and/or transform the main character (emotion) over time in a meaningful way (theme). The degree of character change or transformation can vary dramatically depending on the genre.

For suspense stories, mysteries, and thrillers, plot is defined as the events that take the protagonist from the darkness of not knowing what is happening to the light of solving the mystery, exposing the killer, or destroying the villain. In these categories of genre fiction, the main character is charged with a specific task that defines each event, serving to transport the character from the chaos of the unknown in the beginning of the story, through the twists and turns of the middle, and all the way to an unexpected outcome at the end.

In action-packed genre stories, the action takes center stage, and the character is in the front row as the doer of the action. Each clue, each step forward, each dead-end, and each step backward leads directly to the next event, which leads to more clues and information that send the character deeper and deeper into the story. In the end, the character learns new skills, uncovers new knowledge, or picks up clues and becomes more confident, though the main emphasis of the story is less on how the character changes internally and more on how the character acts externally to bring the story to a successful conclusion.

Conversely, in literary fiction, women's fiction, fantasy, and horror, plot is more nuanced. Rather than following a step-by-step linear progression of events, the protagonist journeys through a more fluid and *seemingly* random chain of events that ultimately leads to an internal change in the character and often to a meaningful transformation. (The word *seemingly* is in italics to remind you that though scenes may appear random to the reader, nothing in a story is random or accidental but rather is deliberately plotted by cause and effect, which we discuss later in this chapter.)

In both cases—in stories driven by action and in stories directed by the character—the conflict and challenges the character encounters on her way toward her goal reveal her emotions. Relationships in both types of stories arouse emotion as well. The display of characters' emotions bonds readers to the story and allows them to not only observe the protagonist draw nearer or further way from her goal(s) but also to experience that character's setbacks and successes emotionally.

No matter what your genre preference, all writers benefit from a firm understanding of the three major plotlines in every good story: action, emotion, and theme.

- Action is physical and concrete.
- Emotion is moving and sensory.
- Theme is cerebral and abstract.

Writing Deep Scenes is divided into three sections to reflect the importance of the three major plotlines found in each and every scene.

ACTION

The action in every kind of story is created by your characters' goals. Goals provide motivation. Obstacles create tension. Potential loss promises transformation. Concrete goals with formidable obstacles and a significant potential for loss create the action of a story. Stated goals stimulate excitement and page-turnability. The action the protagonist takes to fulfill her goals forces her to stretch and grow toward her ultimate transformation.

To generate action, it is vital that the character's long-term goals be tangible rather than abstract. "To be happy" is a general, abstract long-term goal that leads to a vague and meandering story. Instead, goals that create action should be *specific*. In other words, what does the protagonist of this story believe she needs (goal) to make her happy?

The long-term goal also needs to be *definable* and *quantifiable*. In other words, in each scene the reader must be able to determine when the character is moving nearer to her goal and when she is drifting further away.

Setting goals for your protagonist demands a clear vision of what the protagonist desires on a concrete, challenging (yet attainable), specific, and measurable basis. These goals must be within the protagonist's capabilities of achieving (though, of course, you will develop all sorts of antagonists, both internal and external, to interfere with her success). The better defined the protagonist's goal at the overall story level and at the scene level, the more grounded the reader will be in the story, because he knows what is at stake and has a vague idea of the direction in which the story is moving. Often the protagonist's goals change or shift after the major turning points in your story. The more challenging the goal, the more exciting the story. A goal gets the character—and the story—moving. This demands action.

A specific and tangible long-term goal generates several short-term goals—the actions the character feels she needs to take to achieve her bigger long-term goal.

Is she going to succeed at accomplishing her goal … or not? Give the protagonist specific short-term steps to answer this question. Let her actions define her and reflect her emotions. A concrete goal puts the protagonist in action, and the reader reacts to what the character *does* rather than merely following her internal monologue.

Give the protagonist something to *do*—something she believes she is incapable of doing but must do for the good of herself as well as of her family and community at large.

EMOTION

The beginning of your story establishes who the character is, flaws and all. Your readers can look back to this portrait and compare it to who she becomes as she undergoes a transformation after the crisis. This portrait also foreshadows who she will be when she reaches the climax in the story.

At the beginning of a story, the character's emotional reactions help identify and introduce her. By the First Energetic Marker (Point of No Return, at the one-quarter mark of a story), all of the protagonist's most defining traits, positive and negative, have been introduced. (More on Energetic Markers later in this chapter.)

The emotions the protagonist managed to keep in check in the beginning of the story begin to unravel in the chaos and uncertainty of the unfamiliar world of the middle. Overwhelmed and fearful, challenged and hurt, she becomes vulnerable. Most important, the middle deepens the reader's appreciation for the protagonist's emotional maturity, or lack thereof, by displaying her emotional reactions to the increasingly difficult obstacles she must surmount.

All the outer events, ordeals, successes, and failures the character experiences constitute the action of a story and provide the catalyst for change. The further the protagonist penetrates into the new world of the middle, and the more obstacles she confronts, the more she is forced to change her course of action or goals. This change is called a reversal.

With every reversal, the character's emotional defenses break down and her emotions become bleaker and darker. Unable to function at a superficial level any longer, she begins to experience heightened emotions, ones that touch the core of her being. When she is prevented from reaching her goal, her emotional reaction changes subtly over time.

One of the defining elements of the final quarter of a story is the number of complications the protagonist is slapped with as she moves nearer to achieving her goal. With each difficulty and impediment, the protagonist suffers yet another reversal. Yet, unlike the reversals in the middle of the story, the protagonist no longer loses power even if she is physically, mentally, or emotionally restrained or injured. As the character's emotional development changes, her emotional expression changes, too. What begins with the display of emotional upheaval transforms into emotional maturity.

At the end of a story, as a result of the action, the character's transformation is revealed through the change in her choices and in her emotional responses as compared to how she acted in the beginning and in the middle.

The plot of a story is about a character faced with a series of conflicts and obstacles while in pursuit of a goal, which over time inspires her to change her choices. In the end, she is transformed, and her ultimate transformation lends her a different understanding of herself and her existence.

A character flaw is often introduced in the beginning of the story, is deepened in the middle as the stakes rise, and trips her up more and more until she can no longer deny her part in her failure. This awareness triggers her ultimate transformation at the end of the story. Each obstacle and antagonist provides the protagonist with opportunities to learn about herself and thus advance her emotional development. Before she can transform, she first must become conscious of her strengths and weaknesses. Stories show characters *changing* at minimum and *transforming* at their most profound. Often you can achieve this profundity by creating a flawed character. Eventually she will have to face that flaw and overcome it to achieve her ultimate goal.

THEME

Every story is made up of themes: words that convey abstract meaning like *justice, loyalty, loss, betrayal, abandonment, love, friendship, acceptance*, and *forgiveness*. The major themes developed and repeated in a story lead readers to an understanding of what all the words add up to. A *thematic significance statement* is the unifying idea in a story and is either stated outright or indirectly.

Thematic significance ties an entire story together. It is the main thrust of the presentation and what the author hopes to prove through his words. It attempts to unite broad universal truths with the specific words used in your individual story and is intended to embody the heart and meaning of the story. It is the *why*: what you want your audience to take away after having read your story. It's the deeper meaning.

A thematic significance statement becomes a sort of touchstone for writers. This statement, which best represents your entire story, serves as a litmus test for evaluating the effectiveness of each scene in relationship to the whole. The thematic significance statement reflects the truth of your story—not necessarily a universal truth or a truth for all time, but a truth for *your* story. This statement may never be directly stated, but it should be implied through the actions, and especially through the symbols, metaphors, and word choices, that appear throughout the story.

The more clearly you can define the themes of your story and the thematic significance, the tighter it will be. Once you have identified your story's thematic significance, your scene choices and word choices follow that theme throughout the story. The theme then serves as your compass, determining what fits and what doesn't.

STORY DESIGN

Though the emphasis on emotion over action, or action over emotion, or meaning over action varies between genres, every story of every genre shares a similar and universal story design. Every story has a beginning, a middle, and an end. Think of the beginning, middle, and end as the containers for your scenes. An understanding of each of these containers, and how they rise to a high point with an expected energetic shift, eases your task as writer because you know what essential elements are needed to satisfy each section. Each of these three parts provides a stable center and coherence for the various plotlines to unfold. And each of these three parts requires individual and significantly different focus and attention.

Writing Deep Scenes divides story design further by breaking the middle (which typically constitutes half of all the scenes in a story) into two equal parts: the emerging middle and the deeper middle. Each of these four major story parts makes up a quarter of the story, and each part functions in uniquely different ways from the others.

- **BEGINNING:** Dwelling in the Shadow Realm
- **EMERGING MIDDLE:** Testing the Self: Brightening and Recommitting
- **DEEPER MIDDLE:** Stretching the Self in Intensifying Darkness
- **END:** Seeing the Light and Completing Integration

The Beginning

The beginning introduces the familiar: characters, habits, the setting, thought patterns, actions. It presents the protagonist's world as she lives it at the beginning of the story. The opening of the story actively draws in the reader through action that creates conflict, tension, suspense, and/or curiosity.

The action in the scenes in the opening quarter of the story culminates to cause a separation, a shift, a fracture. The effect? The protagonist leaves everything behind at the First Energetic Marker, or Point of No

Return, and crosses into the middle. Action in the beginning creates the pace of a story and determines the level of story excitement. Thematic details in the beginning hint at the meaning of the piece.

This universal design, in which the beginning encompasses one quarter of the story, gives the writer just enough pages and scene opportunities to establish everything the reader needs to know in order to enter the middle. A beginning that extends beyond one-quarter causes readers to grow tired of the introductions. They want something big to happen. They want to be swept off their feet.

The First Energetic Marker gives the reader this promise. A shift or reversal in scene outside the character sends her into the heart of the story world.

The Emerging Middle

Directly after the First Energetic Marker (Point of No Return), the protagonist leaves behind the life she knows in favor of the unknown. New and challenging situations arise. Self-doubts and uncertainty confront the character. She discovers strengths and struggles with shortcomings. The character becomes more and more conscious of her thoughts, feelings, actions, and the life she has always known.

A band of antagonists controls the emerging middle: other people, nature, society, machines, and the inner demons of the character herself. The actions of the antagonists interfere with the protagonist getting what she wants and serve as roadblocks to her ultimate success. The antagonists' rhythmic waves of assault spur the protagonist's emotions in the unfamiliar world of the middle. Relentless challenges cause the protagonist to falter and question her decisions.

The emerging middle ends with the Second Energetic Marker, Rededication, as the protagonist recommits to her goal.

The Deeper Middle

The deeper middle is the second half of the middle and involves darker actions and darker emotions as the protagonist moves ever nearer to the Third Energetic Marker, Dark Night. The scene(s) of highest intensity in the story so far occur here.

Meddlesome, murky, and *sagging* are words often used to describe the middle of an early draft of a novel, memoir, or screenplay. One way to support the deeper middle is to provide an overarching tension: Will she or won't she succeed at achieving her goals? When the reader is clear that something significant is at stake, like life or death, he turns the pages faster.

The nearer the protagonist is to reaching her goal, the more fiercely the antagonists work to prevent her, which creates tension and excitement. This back-and-forth between protagonist and antagonists forms the essential, dynamic yin and yang of stories.

All the rules, customs, expectations, and punishments of this new setting of the deeper middle reflect the antagonist's world. To be successful, the protagonist must master these challenges. The primary function of the deeper middle is to induce change. As such, it is a place of struggle and resistance.

As long as the protagonist resists, and until she accepts what is, she suffers. In each of the scenes in the deeper middle, she continues using techniques that used to always work and never failed her in her old world. These techniques prove useless in the unknown world of the deeper middle.

Toward the end of the deeper middle, a betrayal or a death changes everything and jolts her awake to her internal flaws, and perhaps to her flawed thinking as it pertains to her goals. All her illusions shatter, and nothing will ever be the same again. The difference between what happens in the deeper middle and every other scene in the middle of your story is the level of intensity. In every other scene in the middle, as the protagonist continues trying and failing, dread and anxiety and self-doubt grow. She becomes even tenser and more restless.

Throughout the deeper middle of a story, antagonists are always more powerful than the protagonist and seem always to find just the right buttons to push to bring out the worst in her. After the threshold following the Dark Night, all of that changes. For now, the antagonist(s) rule.

The End

In the last quarter of the story, the protagonist struggles to take full ownership of her newly discovered consciousness. It starts as a twinge, but in the quick buildup to the Fourth Energetic Marker, Triumph, the protagonist recognizes more and more, and quite painfully each time, that her actions or speech do not align with her new understanding of herself and the world around her.

The fabulous beginning of a story and the wild twists in the middle do not count nearly as much to a reader as the end of the story. Readers are affected first and foremost emotionally, whether the story evokes fear and anger, joy and celebration, or sadness and resignation. Connecting with readers emotionally to the point where they become instinctively involved in the story is the dream of every writer. The best place to search for this emotional effect is at the Triumph.

The end sets up the crowning glory of the entire story at the Fourth Energetic Marker. Here the character is fully united with her new self-knowledge, new understanding of the world, and new sense of responsibility as shown through her actions and her words.

Combining Emotion, Action, and Meaning with Story Design

Excitement, suspense, mystery, and page-turnability intensify as you travel deeper into a story. Tying all the parts together is a throughline of scenes showing action, emotion, and meaning at each of the four major turning points, the Energetic Markers. These four fixed points mark the story's rise and fall further into the unknown.

Each one of these major markers is designed to create a plot that carries the reader from the beginning to the end of your story. While writing and rewriting the final quarter of the story and the climax itself, a writer looks hard at the meaning of things. An exploration of deep-rooted ideas for the fundamental meaning of events reveals thematic significance, which in turn dictates the final layer in the selection, organization, nuances, and details of the story.

Stories that get readers thinking resonate with meaning. Stories that expose readers to new ideas and vicarious encounters create opportunities for a shared experience with others. A promising story with a thematically rich climax encourages the reader to ponder the deeper meaning and, in that way, is sure to deliver success.

ENERGETIC MARKERS

Energetic markers are the four key "fixed positions" at the design level of the entire story: Point of No Return, Rededication, Dark Night, and Triumph. They are called Energetic Markers because, like in a musical performance where a gradual increase in the loudness of a sound or section of music crescendos, the energy of the story gradually increases as the scenes begin to reach the four key markers. This gradual increase peaks in the scene or section of scenes that play out at the Energetic Markers.

The four Energetic Markers occur in the following places:

- **AT THE ONE-QUARTER MARK:** Point of No Return
- **AT THE HALFWAY MARK:** Rededication
- **AROUND THE THREE-QUARTER MARK:** Dark Night
- **NEAR THE END MARK:** Triumph

In high-action stories and lots of screenplays, the first two Markers—Point of No Return and Rededication—nearly always arrive at the one-quarter mark and the halfway mark, respectively. The scene and page count of the last two Markers—Dark Night and Triumph—can vary depending on genre and story needs.

These four spots occupy the same placement in all, or almost all, stories, forming a universal design that you'll find in best-selling literature and screenplays because it speaks to something deeply resonant in human experience. A significant change occurs in the dramatic action of your story for your characters, and in the story's meaning at each of these critical and pivotal turning points. Once you learn the power and placement of each of these key positions, you'll be able to organize your stories for greatest impact.

Recommended Scene Types at Each Energetic Marker

Though these key turning points remain fixed and are often conveyed with the use of specific scene types, learning to vary your scene types brings depth, tension, and texture to your story. (We describe scene types in chapter three.) For instance, a contemplative scene, a lay-of-the-land scene, or a resolution scene in and around the Dark Night Energetic Marker serves to dampen and dull the impact rather than to increase the intensity of the excitement and energy at the highest point in the story so far.

First Energetic Marker: Point of No Return

The Point of No Return is a powerfully fraught moment in the story for your protagonist. The marker that represents the Point of No Return for the character can be played out in one or more scenes.

The protagonist makes a choice based on the events of the first quarter of her story and steps out of her shadow world.

Some of the scene types we recommend at the Point of No Return include:

- first scenes
- suspense scenes

- transition scenes
- twister scenes
- escape scenes
- chase scenes

Second Energetic Marker: Rededication

Always marking the end of the emerging middle, the Rededication appears before the deeper middle and is the most powerful recommitment scene in your story, a place where the protagonist looks past fears and doubts, and pushes forward despite not knowing what the outcome will be. The recommitment scene at the Rededication establishes where the character is at the halfway point of the story in relation to the action and the character's emotions, too.

Some of the scene types we recommend at the Rededication Marker include:

- recommitment scenes
- lay-of-the-land scenes
- twister scenes
- dialogue scenes
- escape scenes
- contemplative scenes
- resolution scenes

Third Energetic Marker: Dark Night

Dark Night is a place of explosive and devastating dramatic action and destruction of the old. It represents the lowest point of your protagonist's journey, a time of crisis, loss, even death, whether a literal death or the death of illusion. The character cannot return to her shadow life or to her old ways. This marker may serve as a wake-up call that changes her emotional development and will effect the dramatic action of the rest of the plot.

Some of the scene types we recommend at the Dark Night Marker include:

- crisis scenes
- twister scenes
- suspense scenes
- dialogue scenes
- epiphany scenes

Fourth Energetic Marker: Triumph

The most powerful climax scene of the novel takes place in the final quarter of the story, at the fourth and final Energetic Marker: Triumph. This is where protagonist and antagonist clash in a most dramatic show of energy. Here the protagonist reclaims the power she relinquished to other people, places, and things. This is her high point, in stark contrast to the low point of her Dark Night. She acts with confidence and emotional maturity. She is empowered, and as such, she is set up to triumph over antagonists to achieve her goals and bring thematic cohesion to the story. This may take place in one or several scenes.

The scene types we recommend at the Triumph Marker include:

- climax scenes
- suspense scenes
- twister scenes
- dialogue scenes

Cause and Effect

A story is made up of scenes with a clear dependence on each other, created by cause and effect. The action in one scene affects the character and causes her to act or react, which causes yet another effect and ties together the story in a meaningful and relevant way. Scenes strung together without this sort of linkage begin to feel episodic, random, superficial, and meaningless to your reader.

Test for cause and effect at the scene level and at the overall design level with the help of the Energetic Markers. Does what happens at the Point of No Return cause or contribute to the Rededication? Does what happens at the Rededication in turn cause or directly influence what happens at the Dark Night? Does what happens at the Dark Night directly affect what happens at the ultimate Triumph?

IN SUMMARY

Plot is how the dramatic events (action) in a story change and/or transform the main character (emotion) over time in a meaningful way (theme). All stories incorporate these defining elements in the form of plotlines that run together from the beginning all the way to the end of the story. Different scene types create different effects, bringing together a fusion of action, character, and theme at different moments in your story. The wide use of the vast array of scene types linked together by cause and effect create a compelling plot.

The four Energetic Markers that fall in each of the four parts of the story (the beginning, emerging middle, deeper middle, and end) occur:

- **AT THE ONE-QUARTER MARK:** Point of No Return
- **AT THE HALFWAY MARK:** Rededication
- **AROUND THE THREE-QUARTER MARK:** Dark Night
- **NEAR THE END MARK:** Triumph

CHAPTER TWO

SCENE OVERVIEW

In order to get the most out of this book, it's necessary to learn, or to refresh your understanding of, what comprises a scene at its most essential level: how it functions, the difference between summary and scene, and how scenes work together in relationship to plot design.

A scene on its own is like one perfect note of music, a beautiful sound that contains all the necessary elements to resonate in the listener's inner ear. And when you add all of the scenes together, you get a magnificent new piece of music—a symphony of sound.

It's helpful to think of your scene, then, as a sound chamber that contains the following elements. In every scene you should find:

- **THE PROTAGONIST AND HER GOALS.**
- **ANTAGONISTS AND ALLIES**—characters to thwart and support her goals.
- **MOMENTUM**—also known as action, which often appears in the form of small actions or dialogue, and creates a sense of movement through time and space. Arguably, if you have no momentum, you have no scene, or, at most, a highly contemplative one.
- **NEW PLOT INFORMATION**—either given as a consequence of the last scene or a new plot goal, so that each scene adds to the last.
- **SETTING AND TIME PERIOD**—revealed in sensory details and perceptions as conveyed through character interactions rather than summary.
- **THEMATIC IMAGERY**—the overarching meaning of your story conveyed in images and sensory details throughout.

- **TENSION**—a feeling of conflict and uncertainty that keeps the reader wanting and guessing. Tension occurs when a writer has paid attention to all three layers—action, emotion, and theme—in every scene.

There's one exception: Chapter three lists a couple of scene types—such as transition scenes or contemplative scenes—that do not need all of the elements of a scene, but the above list contains the essential ingredients.

SCENE DESIGN

Scenes are microcosms of your larger plot. Each scene (comprised of the ingredients above) takes us into a crucial moment of your characters' story and should engage both our emotions and our minds by creating real-time momentum or action. If you've never thought much about the shape of a scene, consider it a self-contained ministory with a rising energy that builds to an epiphany, a discovery, an admission, an understanding, or an experience. The reader should feel as though every scene has purpose, deepens character, drives the story forward, and ends in such a way that he just has to know what happens next.

Scenes don't so much begin as *launch*—often in the midst of an event or activity. That is to say, you need not start scenes with an explanation or exposition but simply with an entrance into the action. Then, by following a character's goals and desires, you walk your reader through a setting—preferably in a way that shows the protagonist interacting with it, not just observing it—employing the character's sensory perceptions, introducing his conflict and relationship with inner and outer antagonists and allies, and building the character to a high or low point. Never leave the reader too satisfied at the end of a scene; she must want to keep reading to find out what happens next.

Each scene creates consequences that must be dealt with or built upon in the next scene. And thus, scene by scene, you tell a compelling story that has the dramatic power and emotional impact of a great piece of music.

A scene is defined by the presence of *more* real-time momentum than interior monologue (contemplation) or expository explanation. Real-time momentum is a combination of action, dialogue, and character interaction with his surroundings and other characters. Scenes crackle with energy and rhythms that make readers feel as though they are right beside (or inside) the character as he experiences any number of situations and scenarios. In contrast, narrative summary—lecturing, explaining, or describing—puts readers to sleep after too long.

Your scenes can end on a high note (a small victory for your character) or a low note (a moment of cliff-hanging suspense or uncertainty). It doesn't matter which way it goes so long as each scene concludes by setting up future conflicts for the character(s) and creating in readers a yearning to know what happens next.

If you're wondering about whether a passage or section you've written qualifies as a scene, consider what scenes are *not*.

- Scenes are not an opportunity to take your character on a long, leisurely detour into situations with characters that have nothing to do with the protagonist's dramatic action goals (that's a character profile or vignette).
- Scenes are not a place to explain something or to lecture to your reader (that's a pace killer).
- Scenes are not long histories of people and places (that's dull backstory).

Scene Versus Summary

Not everyone understands the difference between scene and summary, so let us provide a clear distinction.

Summary explains something to the reader. It offers information, ranging from long-winded histories of the town your character lives in to pat descriptions or rambling explanations for a character's behavior. Summary doesn't engage the senses, and it rarely involves moment-by-moment action.

Examples of summary include:

- "It was a beautiful day." (Show this beauty in visual description instead. Is the sun shining? Is the air cool on her skin?)
- "She felt happy for the first time in months." (Demonstrate her happiness through actions, dialogue, exchanges with other characters, and internal sensory perceptions of her body. How does happiness feel? What do happy people do? Say? Think?)
- "He told her about what the surgery would involve, how she would feel, and what the recovery time looked like." (Use active dialogue to reveal the specifics that the character and the reader need to know.)
- "She didn't trust men because her father had been the one to leave her all alone in the boat that night, when she almost drowned, and she now also had a terrible fear of water." (You can show her mistrust of men in her actions. She can tell someone about this event from her past, or you could use a flashback scene to show it unfolding at a dramatic point in the story.)

Alongside action, scenes exist when there are observable sensory perceptions within the protagonist that evoke emotion in the reader and a sense of momentum in space and time.

When to Use Summary

We aren't unreasonable about the purpose of summary in scenes or as transitions between them. You can get away with using summary in scenes in a few places:

- **CONDENSING TIME:** When you need to change the time in a scene, you certainly don't need to make your characters wait on the beach while you bring the sun down, describing every color change in the sky. To condense time, you can simply write, "Night fell," or "Six hours passed," or "A month later." These are appropriate segues that don't require further explanation.

- **CHANGING OR CONDENSING LOCATIONS:** Readers don't need to see every storefront your character passes on her drive from one place to another. They don't care how many red lights she goes through (unless she blows through them—that detail might be noteworthy). In other words, as with time, you have full license to get people where they're going without any preamble or further description: "They walked three miles to her mother's house," or "The train took them a hundred miles closer to their destination," or "They drove back to her apartment."
- **REITERATING DETAILS PREVIOUSLY REVEALED IN THE STORY:** This is actually a very important and handy trick. Let's say the reader witnesses an event that takes place earlier in the narrative in scene form. Later, one of the characters in that scene needs to tell another character what happened. Rather than have the character repeat all the actions, you can simply summarize: "I told him about the events leading up to the explosion," or "She recounted the high points of the battle," or "She told him everything she could remember about the abduction."

Demonstrate, Don't Lecture

Rather than citing the commonly used adage "Show, don't tell," a more helpful direction for scene work is "Demonstrate, don't lecture." If you tell the reader a character is "outraged," you're lecturing. Where's the proof? Demonstrate her outrage in action and dialogue. Don't lecture us about your character's wounded backstory; demonstrate her wounds through how she behaves, thinks, and speaks. Instead of using summary to rehash discoveries and epiphanies, keep them front and center—onstage—so that the reader experiences these moments with the character.

A fun phrase for remembering the functions of a scene is "A scene is a stylized, sharper simulacrum of reality."

- **STYLIZED:** Nothing in your scene appears by accident; you have crafted every moment, every interaction, and every image. To the reader something may seem benign, but you know nothing is.
- **SHARPER SIMULACRUM:** We read to experience a heightened, more fulfilling version of real life, with all the boring bits excised. In your bid to create a realistic experience, don't put every single action—the mundane, dull, insignificant moments and boring pleasantries of real life—into your scenes. Include only those that lend themselves to character and plot development and are rich with tension and suspense, those that contribute to the feeling of not knowing how things will play out in the character's favor or if antagonists will prevail.

Following are some examples of scenes—or "scenelets," for our purposes, as these are not full scenes but have all the key ingredients that tell a reader a scene is unfolding: action (look to the verbs if you're unsure what qualifies as action), dialogue (spoken words), and sensory imagery (invoking the five senses) that create immediacy, momentum, and the sense that events are unfolding in the "now." Note that in a screenplay it's easy to recognize when you're in a scene because movies progress predominantly in scenes, unless you hear a voiceover (a character who narrates story over the images). However, in literature we rely on the key ingredients of scene to inform us that we are in one, as you will see in these examples.

> They were moving quickly now, Wolgast at the wheel, Doyle beside him, thumbing away furiously on his handheld. Calling in to let Sykes know who was in charge.
> "No goddamn signal." Doyle tossed his handheld onto the dash. They were fifteen miles outside of Homer, headed due west; the open fields slid endlessly away under a sky thick with stars.
> —from *The Passage*, an apocalyptic vampire novel by Justin Cronin

> Her hands flew through the scalded feathers, plucking each one until a gray snow pile drifted at her feet and began to swirl in the breeze.

Mabel singed the skin with matches, sulfur rising from each filament, an acrid incense. She dragged on a Lucky.

"You dassn't go saying bad things about the Doctor." My grandmother's cigarette bobbed at me, its orange ember blowing like a hazard light.

—from *Daughter of the Queen of Sheba,* a memoir by Jacki Lyden

It was dark when Lewis jolted awake. The woods seemed to be moving around them. He turned to Rose, who was sleeping, one arm thrown over his chest. As soon as he moved, her eyes flew open. She jolted up and started brushing the twigs from her skirt. "Hurry," he said.

—from *Is This Tomorrow,* a novel by Caroline Leavitt

Scene Types

In this chapter, we've given you a basic recipe for scenes, and in chapter three we'll take you deep into our comprehensive list of scene types. For now, just keep in mind that not all scenes have the same effect inside a story—some are designed to slow the pace (contemplative scenes, for instance), while others bring the energy up (suspense scenes and twister scenes, for instance). While you may not use all the scene types, learning how to write different kinds of scenes will, however, make your writing sing in new and valuable ways. For instance, there are some scene types that, at the different fixed positions of your character's development and story design, are necessary to meet the demands of your character's plot goals, as well as to keep the energy of your story high. Others can be woven in to twist your character's emotion or plot goals and to conjure or maintain suspense. Mixing up your scene types will make your story robust and memorable.

Shadow and Light

We talk a lot about the elements of shadow and light in this book. The shadow realm refers to your character's inner life—her feelings, thoughts, and opinions; her backstory; and all that is unknown to her (whether by her denial or the design of your story) as well as the thematic elements that reflect these states. These shadow parts of herself are those she may be unable to look at or to see at the beginning, which trip her up or get her into trouble: her flaws, her immaturity, her selfish desires. The shadow emotions and backstory will manifest themselves in scenes in her actions and dialogue: She may make unwise decisions or say foolish things. She will act out her shadow moment by moment.

The more your character undergoes change and transformation throughout your story, the more her emotional life moves toward the light of integration; in other words, she gets to know herself, sees herself more clearly, overcomes her flaw(s), masters new skills, and finds inner resources she will need to triumph and achieve her goals. Thus she will begin to behave, think, and speak in a more integrated manner the further into the story you go, until at last she emerges through trial and triumph, into the light of her own power. These sorts of journeys require shifts in awareness, epiphanies, new understandings, and losses and challenges.

You will plant thematic imagery, symbols, metaphor, and analogies in your scenes (we address such things in Part Three of the book) that reflect and represent what stage or aspect of the shadow or light your character embodies.

ACTION, EMOTION, AND THEME

We've divided this book into three sections, which correspond with the key elements of any good story: action, emotion, and theme. It may seem as though we are suggesting that you write separate scenes for each of these key elements, but all three are integral and must be present in every scene. Think of them as layers, like three notes in a perfume: a top note that gives a first impression, and a middle layer that gives way to a base note that grounds the scent. The same is true with the elements in a scene, though they are more braided together than layered on top of one another.

You will quickly be able to identify which layer you have the most comfort writing and which layer or layers you struggle with. There are, for instance, writers who inherently understand action; their stories are full of quick, detailed events, but their characters might ring a little hollow or flat. Other writers are better at the workings of emotions and develop their characters' inner lives and relationships with ease but may struggle to figure out what happens next.

We find, however, that it is easier for writers to comprehend each element if we break them out separately to hold up to the light and inspect. By teasing them apart at the scene level, like layers of a carbon copy, you will be able to see the pattern beneath the design and then fuse them together as a unified tapestry when you work on your own story.

Generating Tension Within Each Scene

Creating tension is a secondary goal of any scene. It is a quality that exists in every scene in which the action, emotion, and theme layers are all working together. Think of the emotional swell that rises in your chest when a powerful symphony begins—all instruments suddenly playing in harmony, the deepest sounds vibrating in your core, the highest notes soaring above you into the atmosphere. In a nutshell, tension is a feeling of *wanting* in the reader: wanting to know what happens next; wanting to fall more deeply under a captivating spell; wanting for a character to free herself from danger, to profess her love, to discover the ancient prophecy, or to resist the antagonist's goals. Sometimes the wanting that readers experience is for a bit more of whatever it is you're doing—they want to prolong the beauty or rapture or magic you've created. Other times they want something to unfold, to be revealed, or to finish up— which speaks to creating suspense.

Tension manifests when the action is tight and builds authentically from the character's goals and desires. It also exists when language is crisp and fresh and twists the reader's inner ear in interesting ways, and when characters have deep, complex, and multilayered emotional experiences rather than acting like one-note stereotypes. It exists when the forces between protagonist and antagonist collide and clash. You'll know you have tension when readers can't put your story down, and when your characters feel like real people.

Keep in mind these three keys to building tension in every scene:

1. **UNCERTAINTY IS PRESENT:** The reader and protagonist do not know exactly what will happen next (even when the character is taking decisive action), keeping both on their toes. You don't have too much predictability.

2. **CHARACTERS HAVE COMPLEX, MULTILAYERED EMOTIONS:** Characters' feelings are never singular: Happiness may come with relief or anger, and sorrow may hold a touch of relief. The more you can demonstrate layers of feelings in every scene, the more tension is wrought within the scene.

3. **FORCES OPPOSE:** Things are never too easy for your protagonist but also never so insurmountably hard that the reader gives up hope. Dialogue pushes and pulls with energy, characters must work for their goals, and antagonists push back with mighty force.

TIPS FOR WHEN YOU'RE STUCK WITHIN A SCENE

Every writer comes to a point (or several) when he feels stuck in a scene. He either (1) becomes stuck inside the action of the scene, uncertain what to do to make it feel purposeful or move forward, or (2) doesn't know which scene to write next.

Let's address (1) first: When you're stuck inside a scene, you've most likely encountered one of the following issues:

- **YOU DON'T KNOW YOUR CHARACTER'S GOAL FOR THE SCENE.** Every scene should build organically from the scene before. Your character needs a goal that sets up a new consequence for the next scene. If you haven't quite firmed up your character's goals, you may find yourself stuck. Go back, determine her goal (often just a "next step" in her plot journey), and then make sure the scene builds toward that goal.

- **YOU'VE MADE IT TOO EASY FOR HER TO REACH HER GOAL.** Good stories, from the quietest literary tale about speaking one's truth to the most epic of journeys to save the universe from evil, are built upon the conflict and trials that stretch and push characters or narrators to grow into their full power and possibility. If your character achieves what she's after without *any* challenge, your scenes will lack tension and feel uneventful, causing readers to lose interest. If this is the case, ask yourself: In what ways can my character's flaws work against her? How can the antagonist post an obstacle or challenge in this scene? What is one way I can make this goal harder for her to obtain in this moment? Remember that challenging characters is one way to push them to marshal inner strength they may not yet be demonstrating in your story. In the case of memoir, you may have to consciously pick scenes that come from more challenging parts of your journey rather than just the "colorful" but easy ones you may have chosen.

- **YOU'VE GIVEN YOUR CHARACTER TOO DIFFICULT AN OBSTA-CLE, THUS PREVENTING HER FROM REACHING HER GOAL WHEN SHE NEEDS TO.** Every obstacle in a story should be, as screenwriter Michael Hauge says, "a seemingly insurmountable" obstacle. This means that while the reader may not, at this moment, see how your character is going to get out of this tough situation, you, the author, have engineered a surprise or twist, possibly involving the character's hidden strength or resourcefulness, the unexpected aid of an ally, or an oversight on the part of the antagonist. However, if you make obstacles too hard, such that your character loses hope or you must rely upon deus ex machina (Latin for "God in the machine," which refers to implausible, easy, or magical fixes to plot obstacles), you stretch plausibility and fatigue your reader. In addition to conquering larger obstacles, your character does need to achieve smaller goals, such as making new friends, journeying to a new land, or taking on a task.

- **YOU DON'T KNOW WHICH SCENE TO WRITE NEXT.** Chapter one, "Plot Overview," gave you some insight into the basic underpinnings of plot in the form of the Energetic Markers, the "fixed positions" or turning points where powerful energy shifts the story (and a character's emotional and spiritual position) in a slightly new direction. Rest assured we will repeat this information over and over from different angles throughout this book, but the most important way to know which scene to write next is to follow the energy of the plot design. Staying true to the Energetic Markers of your story cuts down drastically on the guesswork. Each scene is simply another milestone on the character's journey toward the next marker, and each phase between markers finds her either more in the shadows or closer to the light. If you launch your story with a strong Point of No Return scene or scenes, your protagonist's beginning will flow organically into her middle. If you understand the purpose of the Rededication Marker, then the middle will not sag but deepen and become more complex, build to a natural Dark Night, and then rise again to a Triumph that makes sense for your protagonist and your story.

IN SUMMARY

Design your plot scene by scene, paying careful attention to the Energetic Markers where the story shifts in a new direction, and invoking sensory experience, tension, and emotional layering. Remember to work in moment-by-moment action, utilize the senses, and demonstrate all key information through character words and deeds.

CHAPTER THREE

SCENE TYPES

We have found, both when working with writers and in our own writing, that it's common for writers to use the same type of scene throughout an entire manuscript. Like a composer using one note in a symphony, or a painter choosing only a single color for a large mural, the effect of using the same scene type for the duration of a novel often creates a flat or monotonous story that doesn't allow your character to undergo a full breadth of transformation.

Even when you know exactly what your story requires, building tension and evoking emotion using a variety of scene designs may elude you. Building a strong, rich, multilayered plot with your scenes and Energetic Markers demands that some scenes be strenuous and complex while others rely on brevity and simplicity. The best scenes are those that accomplish many story demands at once. Still, not all scenes are equal.

We invite you to explore, choose from, and experiment with the vast panoply of scene types featured in this chapter. We have organized them around the universal plot design, walking you through each scene type to remove the guesswork. Our list is by no means exhaustive. However, we find it's a good place to start when looking for the best possible means of entertaining your readers and satisfying the universal expectations for every story.

Using all fifteen types of scenes broadens your ability to reach and impact your readers in the exact way you desire. By integrating a variety of scene types into your stories, you lead the reader deeper into the heart of your action, emotion, and meaning.

MAIN SCENE TYPES

Each scene type may be used anywhere in your story, except where we caution you otherwise, and in various combinations with other scene types. (The following list is in alphabetical order.)

1. Climax Scenes

While the Triumph is the one true climax of the entire story, you may have a mini-climax in a scene of recommitment or epiphany, where the protagonist feels momentarily victorious over the darkness, doubt, or fears that have troubled her. Climax scenes:

- build in intensity.
- contain the highest stakes in the entire story.
- show the protagonist facing her fear and/or foe and prevailing.
- may bring about a temporary reprieve or sense of triumph over an obstacle or situation.
- allow the protagonist to see strengths and resources that may have been hidden from her.

The following is a scene from the contemporary novel *Beautiful Ruins* by Jess Walter, in which three stories run parallel to one another. This scene comes from the past story, from the perspective of the character Pasquale Tursi, an Italian whose life is changed the day a beautiful American actress comes to stay at his humble hotel. By the time this scene occurs, he has been bullied by mobsters for too long and has endured many other terrible things, one after the other. He has reached a place where emotion and action collide into climax.

> Still forty meters apart, with the fading sun right behind them now, Pasquale couldn't make out the looks on the men's faces, just their silhouettes. He said nothing, simply walked, his mind roiling with images of Richard Burton and Michael Deane, of his aunt poisoning his mother, of Amadea and his baby, of his failed tennis court, of his

flinching before Gualfredo last time, of the truth revealed about himself: his core weakness as a man.

"The Brit skipped out on his bar bill," Gualfredo said, now twenty meters away. "You might as well pay me for that, too."

"No," Pasquale said simply.

"No?" Gualfredo asked.

Behind him, he heard Alvis Bender come out onto the patio. "Everything okay down there, Pasquale?"

Gualfredo looked up at the hotel. "And you have another American guest? What are you running here, Tursi? I'm going to have to double the tax."

Pasquale reached them just at the point where the trailhead met the edge of the piazza, where the dirt of the shore blended into the first cobblestone *strada*. Gualfredo was opening his mouth to say something else, but before he could, Pasquale swung the cane. It cracked against the bull neck of the brute Pelle, who apparently wasn't expecting this, perhaps because of Pasquale's sheepish demeanor the last time. The big man lurched to the side and fell in the dirt like a cut tree, Pasquale lifting the cane to swing it again … but finding it broken off against the big man's neck. He threw the handle aside and went after Gualfredo with his fists.

But Gualfredo was an experienced fighter. Ducking Pasquale's haymaker, he landed two straight, compact blows—one to Pasquale's cheek, which burned, and the next to his ear, which caused a dull ringing and sent him reeling backward into the fallen Pelle. Realizing that his own furious adrenaline was a limited resource, Pasquale leapt back at Gualfredo's sausage-packed frame, until he was inside those direct punches, swinging wildly himself, his own blows landing on Gualfredo's head with deep melon *thunks* and light slaps: wrists, fists, elbows—everything he had.

But then the big lamb-shank hand of Pelle landed on his hair and a second meaty hand fell on his back and he was dragged away, and for the first time it occurred to Pasquale that this might not go his way, that he'd likely need more than adrenaline and a broken cane to pull this off. Then even the adrenaline was gone, and Pasquale made a soft, whimpering noise, like a crying child who has exhausted himself. And, like a steam shovel out of nowhere, Pelle slammed a fist into Pasquale's gut, lifting him and dropping him flat to the ground, slumped over, not a molecule of air left anywhere in the world to breathe.

Big Pelle stood over him, a deep frown on his face, framed with the specks of Pasquale's vision as he gasped and waited for the steam shovel to finish them off. Pasquale bent forward and scratched at the dirt below him, wondering why he couldn't smell the sea air but knowing there would be no smelling as long as there was no air. Pelle made the slightest move toward him and then a shadow flashed across the sun and Pasquale looked up to see Alvis Bender fly from the rock wall onto the massive back of Pelle, who hesitated for a moment (he looked like a student with a guitar case strung over his shoulder) before reaching behind himself and tossing off the tall, thin American like a wet rag, sending him skittering across the rocky shore.

2. Contemplative (or Sequel) Scenes

Often a slower, internal scene is needed in reaction to the external events of the narrative. Also known as a sequel scene, a contemplative scene comes after a dramatic, suspense, or epiphany scene, giving the protagonist time to assess how he feels, reassess his goals, and create new strategies in light of all that has happened to him. A contemplative scene:

- often works best as an internal scene between two action scenes.
- shows the character's emotional reaction to his failure or success in the previous scene.
- is as short or as long as necessary for the character to decide what to do next after a particularly trying time.
- provides emotional context for the external action.
- has a higher ratio of interior monologue (thought and rumination about previous action) than of new action or dialogue.
- moves at a slower pace to allow the reader to get a deeper, more intimate look into the protagonist's "inner life."
- contains more of the protagonist's interactions with himself and the setting than with other characters.

- allows the protagonist time to digest actions, events, and epiphanies that have come before and to decide how to act next.
- can be a good place to point more directly to themes of the story through character reflection.
- gives pause before or after an intense scene so that the character can reflect and the reader can catch her breath.

In the novel *Shine, Shine, Shine* by Lydia Netzer, Sunny, the wife of an astronaut who is in space, is pregnant with their second child and has just learned that her mother, who has been in a coma for some time, has passed away in the night. The contemplative scene that follows is a journey into her mind while she is at the hospital about to sign the papers to release her mother's body. She is letting this death sink in, probing her feelings, and reflecting on what will come next.

> There is a real elevation of the conversation, when death and birth come into it. Nothing is unspoken. Everything underneath comes out, and the darkness spills up into the everyday language. You talk about dark things because you have decisions that need to be made. There is no subtlety when you have to decide between cremation and burial, or tell someone whether or not you want to be sedated through it all.
>
> There was a moment, when Sunny was sitting at a small, cheap desk at the hospital, on a rolling office chair, when she forgot her mother's maiden name. Then she knew she was coming unhinged. But she kept signing paperwork anyway, kept the pen going across the paper. In the normal course of your life, do you have any dealings with the coroner? No. Do you have any reason to say the word "autopsy"? Never.
>
> As an orphan, you are alone. There is no one on the Earth watching, when you say, "Look at me!" There is no one standing in the gap between you and oblivion, putting up her hands, and saying, "Stop." You have come this far surrounded, and now you must continue without defense. As a pregnant person, Sunny had to hide herself from this exposure. She had to protect the baby from this distress. So as her mother's ship disappeared, sinking below the horizon, and her own ship sailed

up into the wind, she had to let it go without fireworks, without search-lights, without a trumpet blast. Almost without remark.

Sunny decided against a funeral. She decided that her mother would be cremated. These things were going to be handled by the guy at the mortuary, and she signed the release form that authorized him to take possession of the body. This transfer would take place somewhere in the bowels of the hospital. Her mother would exit out of the back of the building. Sunny did not know what her mother would look like, at that point. It could be really terrible.

There could have been a funeral in Yates County, where all of Emma's friends could attend. There could have been a funeral in Virginia. But Sunny could not arrange a funeral now. She knew her mother would say, "Whatever makes it easier for you, dearest. Do whatever you need to do. I don't care." So her mother would be cremated. It all seemed so impossible that she wanted to tell the mortician to check carefully and be sure her mother was dead. She wanted to install a brightly colored button on the inside of the kiln: "If you are alive and being wrongfully cremated, PRESS HERE." It had been so slow, this dying. Maybe it was not completely done, in spite of what the doctors said. Maybe there were still some synapses firing, some spirit to be res-urrected and intone the words "Good job, Sunny. You are great. You are handling this really well."

"Are you doing okay back there?" a nurse asked her. She had been given two black pens with which to sign all the papers. A pen and a backup pen. But the first pen had worked just fine.

"I'm done, I think," Sunny said. "I think I'm done."

3. Crisis Scenes

Different genres demand that you fling different levels of intensity at the protagonist. In thrillers, suspense, and horror, the protagonist often suffers many mini-crisis scenes where she fails and feels as though she will never make her way toward her goal again. Recommitment scenes often follow crisis scenes once the protagonist figures out how to over-come. The crisis scene of greatest magnitude strikes around the end of the middle—the Dark Night, detailed in chapter two. Keep these considerations in mind when writing crisis scenes:

- The protagonist's crisis is often the antagonist's triumph.
- This is the point of the story when all feels lost; it is the darkest moment for the protagonist in the entire story.
- A crisis scene contains a breakdown that inspires a breakthrough.
- It shows the protagonist at her worst.
- She fails (though it will be only a temporary failure, or the failure will be followed by a success later on).
- Crisis scenes rely on imagery and sensory description to infuse thematic significance, since crises are often heavily symbolic moments.

This crisis scene is from Ariel Gore's memoir, *The End of Eve*, after she and her partner, Sol, have sold their home in Portland. They move their young son, Maxito, to New Mexico to live with her emotionally abusive mother as she is dying of cancer, because it's the right thing to do. Her mother behaves erratically and treats Ariel and her family badly, and as Ariel reaches the end of her rope, the memoir dips into a crisis.

> "How are you doing?" I asked her when she shuffled into the kitchen.
>
> She put a pot of water on to boil. "I'm dying, I'm sure you're happy to know." And then, "I don't know what your family is doing here in my house."
>
> I didn't know what to say. *Your family. My house.* I was tired of this shit, tired of making excuses for her, tired of blaming the tumors or anything else. And it wasn't true that she couldn't help the way she was. She didn't treat everyone this way. She was just an abusive bitch who happened to have cancer. I shook my head, looked right at her. "If anyone in your life has ever treated you like family, it's been me and my kids. If you can't see that, take it up with God."
>
> As I turned away, I heard her low whisper: "You just made a big mistake."
>
> I crawled into bed even though the sliver of a moon had barely risen. I thought I'd read or write, but I just took a few good sips of bourbon

from the bottle on my nightstand and fell asleep. Didn't wake when Sol and Maxito came in.

In the morning, I made coffee and hot cocoa. I scrambled an egg for Maxito. I didn't see my mother. Didn't hear her in her room. Didn't hear the laundry running. We took Maxito to preschool and went to work at the shop, but it was cold and snowy and no one came in so we closed early, picked Maxito up from preschool early and headed home.

As we turned onto the dirt road, Sol gasped, "What the mother?"

Twenty-seven giant black garbage bags in the driveway, our red couch behind them. The grandmother clock. My old hobo bird painting propped against the turquoise trailer.

"Watch *Bell, Book and Candle* again!" Maxito cheered from his car seat.

"Hang on, Maxito." Sol pulled over and I climbed out of the car, blast of cold air and the sound of my own boots on the gravel. I tried the front door, but the front door was locked. My key didn't work. That's when I noticed the living room windows were all boarded up. I walked around the side of the house. My mother's bedroom was the only one not boarded. It was open, and there she was in her green Patagonia jacket, just staring out the window, the screen between us.

"What's going on, Mom?"

She kept staring like I wasn't standing there on the other side.

"Mom, what are you going to do?"

She was quiet at first, didn't move except to smile at a question like that. "Don't worry about me," she finally said. "The devil takes care of his own."

4. Dialogue Scenes

Dialogue scenes move the story forward by having two or more characters communicate with each other and reveal key plot information or deepen character development. These scenes reveal nuances about the characters by what they say and don't say, and what others say about them, and are often perceived as "action" by the reader because they create a sense of momentum. (However, be careful not to use dialogue to dump plot information in a passive way.) Dialogue scenes:

- should reveal and/or deepen character(s).
- are often rapid-paced, which keeps action high.
- reveal plot information that can't be revealed another way, without relying on exposition.
- provide backstory in digestible bites. (Backstory information is doled out in gradual pieces and as necessary to advance the reader's understanding of the character.)
- create real-time action when bigger actions or events are not likely or applicable.
- depict two or more characters opening up beyond the simple exchange of verbal information. This will provide insight into what's really affecting them about the interaction and to point to thematic significance.
- include the emotional significance of the interaction to the character(s).
- include the personal, and often conflicting, agendas (goals) of each character (what he or she hopes to convey or achieve through this exchange of words).

In Ruth Ozeki's novel *A Tale for the Time Being*, protagonist Ruth, a middle-aged writer, finds a diary washed up on the shore of the island where she lives. The writer of the journal is a sixteen-year-old Japanese girl, Nao, who recounts her harrowing tale of being uprooted from the United States and being bullied at school in Japan, as well as the story of her great-grandmother, a 104-year-old Zen Buddhist nun. However, the novel is really about Ruth—how she is handling her own middle age and regrets. In this dialogue scene between her and her husband, we learn more about the character: that Ruth often stands in her own way, and that her biggest lesson is learning to accept the life she already has.

Not knowing is hard. In the earthquake and the tsunami, 15,854 people died, but thousands more simply vanished, buried alive or sucked back out to sea by the outflow of the wave. Their bodies were never found. Nobody would ever know what happened to them. This was the harsh reality of this world, at least.

"Do you think Nao is alive?" Ruth asked.

"Hard to say. Is death even possible in a universe of many worlds? Is suicide? For every world in which you kill yourself, there'll be another in which you don't, in which you go on living. Many worlds seem to guarantee a kind of immortality ..."

She grew impatient then. "I don't care about other worlds. I care about this one. I care whether she's dead or alive in this world. And I want to know how her diary and the rest of the stuff washed up here, on the island." She held out her arm and pointed to the sky soldier watch. "This watch is real. Listen. It's ticking. It's telling me the time. So how did it get here?"

He shrugged. "I don't know."

"I really thought I would know by now," she said, getting to her feet. "I thought if I finished the diary, the answers would be there or I could figure it out, but they weren't, and I can't. It's really frustrating."

But there was nothing she could do about it, and it was time to go upstairs and get back to work. As she reached into the cone to scratch Pesto's head, a thought occurred to her. "That cat of Schrödinger's," she said. "It reminds me of you. What quantum state were you in when you were hiding in the box of the basement?"

"Oh," he said. "That. Definitely smeared. Half-dead and half-alive. But if you'd found me, I would have died, for sure."

"Well, it's a good thing I didn't go looking for you."

He laughed. "Really? You mean that?"

"Of course. What do you think? That I want you dead?"

He shrugged. "Sometimes I think you'd have been better off without me. You could have married a captain of industry and had a nice life in New York City. Instead you're stuck with me on this godforsaken island with a bad cat. A bald bad cat."

"Now you're the one practicing revisionist history," she said. "Is there any evidence to support this?"

"Yes. There's plenty of evidence to prove the cat is very bad. And very bald."

"I'm talking about me being better off without you."

"I don't know. I guess not."

"Well, then, you should wear the Cone of Shame for even suggesting it. Because now you've gone and sentenced me to another life in another world in New York, with some boorish corporate oligarch of a husband. Thanks a lot." She gave the cat a final pat on the nose.

"Well, don't worry," he said. "You've already forgotten all about me."

He was joking, of course, but his words hurt her feelings. She withdrew her hand. "I have not."

He reached across the counter and took her wrist. "I was just kidding," he said, and then he held on a little longer so she couldn't pull away. "Are you happy?" he asked. "Here in this world?"

Surprised, she stood there and thought about his question. "Yes, I suppose I am. At least for now."

5. Epiphany Scenes

An epiphany scene depicts an event that breaks open the heart and mind of the character, revealing his part in his own failures and forcing him into a new understanding of himself. Often a crisis scene creates an ensuing epiphany scene, where the character begins to grasp his dark or weak side. That understanding ultimately contributes to an emotionally fulfilling change and/or transformation at the end of the book. Epiphany scenes come with the following considerations:

- The protagonist gains surprising, new insights, "awakens" to an element(s) of himself he has been oblivious to, and/or breaks through denial.
- This understanding is revealed in a new and very clear way, which will directly affect choices and decisions he makes going forward.

- Epiphany scenes often follow crises because loss and pain can lead to personal growth and change with which readers deeply connect.
- Often a series of epiphany scenes are necessary before the character can truly begin to get out of his own way and reach victory.
- After the awakening of the epiphany, the character begins his character arc transformation by thinking and acting differently.
- As a result of the epiphany, the protagonist is forced to make some sort of choice or change.
- The epiphany either comes at some kind of cost or renews hope and faith.
- The epiphany rises out of plot events and information—it does not come out of the blue.
- The knowledge, understanding, and new insights gained reflect important theme elements.

In Emily St. John Mandel's post-apocalyptic novel *Station Eleven*, this epiphany scene comes, as epiphanies often do, when the characters finally take a moment to pause from or reflect on the dramatic action that has been pushing them forward. Two characters, August and Kirsten, have stopped to rest. Both are members of a traveling symphony that performs music and Shakespearean plays while traveling around the continent, twenty years after a pandemic flu destroyed most of civilization. Their symphony recently encountered an odd town where the members have strange tattoos upon their cheeks and do the bidding of a man named The Prophet. They also are threatened with death if they attempt to leave. August's epiphany at the end of this chapter means more to the reader than to the character at this point. When he comes to it, the reader knows, at last, who The Prophet is.

> They dragged their suitcases down the embankment to the road. They were very close to Severn City now. At twilight the road curved back to the lakeshore, and the first houses of Severn City appeared. Young birch trees between the road and the lake but otherwise no forest, just

overgrown lawns and houses submerged in vines and shrubbery, a beach of rocks and sand.

"I don't want to do this at night," August said. They chose a house at random, waded through the backyard and made camp behind a garden shed. There was nothing to eat. August went exploring and came back with blueberries.

"I'll take the first watch," Kirsten said. She was exhausted but she didn't think she could sleep. She sat on her suitcase, her back against the wall of the shed, a knife in her hands. She watched the slow rise of fireflies from the grass and listened to the water on the beach across the road, the sighing of wind in the leaves. A beating of wings and the squeak of a rodent, an owl making a kill.

"Remember that man we met at the gas station?" August asked. She'd thought he was asleep.

"Of course. What about him?"

"That scar on his face." He sat up. "I was just thinking about it, and I realized what it is."

"The prophet marked him." The memory was agitating. She flicked her wrist and her knife split the cap of a white mushroom a few feet away.

"Yes, but the symbol itself, the pattern of the scar. How would you describe it?"

"I don't know," she said, retrieving her knife. "It looked like a lowercase *t* with an extra line through the stem."

"A shorter line. Toward the bottom. Think about it. It isn't abstract."

"I *am* thinking about it. It looked abstract to me."

"It's an airplane," August said.

6. Escape Scenes

Characters get into jams in many forms of fiction. Genre works often show characters escaping from more dramatic scenarios as the protagonist flees for her life or from a false accusation. Yet it's not uncommon even in memoir and literary fiction to find a character in need of escape. Escaping puts the protagonist on the offensive. Escape scenes:

- are found more commonly in the middle and end scenes, unless your book begins with a character in a state of lockdown or entrapment of some kind.
- depict the protagonist's escape as challenging and often perilous.
- create emotional duress and stress for the protagonist.
- build concern and anxiety in the reader for your protagonist's welfare.
- create a sense of urgency, as the reader becomes anxious that the protagonist will not escape "in time" for something important.
- are heavy on action and leave little time for contemplation.
- show characters moving through a physical location with an emphasis on setting details.
- rely heavily on sensory impressions.
- are combined with suspense scenes to build heightened tension and emotional drama.
- can also act as transition scenes to get your character from one key place to another in a tense or suspenseful way.

In Karen Russell's *Swamplandia!*, young Ava, whose family runs a gator-wrestling theme park in Florida, has willingly gone off into the swamps on a journey with someone who calls himself the Bird Man. The Bird Man claims to be able to take her to "the underworld," where her sister, Ossie, allegedly disappeared with a ghost. Ava's mother recently died, her father has gone AWOL, her brother is off to make it in the world, and young Ava, lacking guidance, is caught up in magical thinking that soon proves dangerous on the journey with the Bird Man. Eventually, after he assaults her, she escapes from him.

> "Ava, I need you to help me over here ..." The Bird Man's voice was full of squishy feeling that sounded to me so much like tenderness, love. Like he really did need me, too. It was a voice you could see, like green glass sparkling in a palm.
>
> At the same time I heard my mother telling me something I should have figured out hours and days ago, something I must have been on the brink of knowing since Stiltsville. I don't mean that my actual

mother told me this, like one of Ossie's ghosts, but it was her voice I heard in my head:

The Bird Man is just a man, honey. He is more lost out here than you are. The Bird Man has no idea where he's taking you, and if he does, well that's much worse, and you won't find your sister anywhere near here, Ava, and I would run, honey, personally …

What I did next was all instinct, as if my muscles were staging a coup: I felt a movement in my breast pocket, the red Seth clawing against the cotton ticking: I pulled her out and untapped her small jaws and flung her at him in one fluid motion. The Bird Man was surprised into reflex. His naked hands flew out like catcher's mitts; I could see past him to where his falconer's gloves were hanging off the keel. He caught the Seth hard against his chest. There was something almost funny about watching this, hysterically funny, but terrifying, too, a bad hilarity that lights up eel-bright in your belly. A hideous squeal went up through the trees but I don't know what happened next, if the red Seth bit him or clawed at him—I was off. I disappeared between two trees and felt my upper body career forward as I slid on the deep peat beds. I caught myself, monkey-swung my way out of a liquidy nick in the limestone. I sucked air on the jumps and splashed through pools of vegetation.

When I got up a little higher I dodged the willow heads and tried to avoid the obvious holes where female gators had piled and clubbed down brush.

Even running, I kept waiting to feel a hand fall onto my shoulder. The only noise I heard was my own progress through the cypress dome, my breath rocket-shipping up and up through a heavy tube of sky.

7. Final Scenes

Your final scene may not even be a full scene but rather a brief glimpse into where your character is or will go at the end of his journey. It is the final taste you leave in the reader's mouth, and many writers choose to end with a powerful image or a thread of philosophy. The final scene:

- provides a snapshot of where your protagonist is now after the conclusion of your plot.
- is often reflective in tone.
- provides a full-circle feeling—by recalling the first scene in some way.
- moves at a slower pace than the middle and end scenes.
- may actually be a cliff-hanger, if your book is part of a series.
- can contain one last surprise, answer, or insight, though this is not necessary.

The final scene of *The Still Point of the Turning World* by Emily Rapp serves as a beautiful ending to a heartbreaking memoir about giving birth to her son, Ronan, who would not live to see his third birthday because of Tay-Sachs disease. Rapp describes a scene that is "part memory, part dream, part wishful thinking"—both a moment of the mourning she knows will come after her son passes and of the beauty and love available in the moments that he is still alive. It's a breathtaking passage that reflects both her grief and the hope for a life beyond grief.

> I am curious and unafraid. My mouth tastes of seawater and wet wool. My feet and legs hurt, but not in an unpleasant way. In fact, I feel sporty and alive. My blood is warm and I can hear my heartbeat, steady and fast but not frantic. The color of the sky begins to change; there is sun behind the thick reach of gray-white clouds. Slowly, it gets warmer and warmer. There are more people on the road now, nodding at me as they pass. The sleepy town is no longer sleeping. I walk down the dirt road, past a yard where baby clothes are fluttering on a clothesline, still too wet and heavy to flap in the wind, which is gentle and sea fragrant. The sun is strong now, almost tropical strength. I reach the shore of a small rocky beach littered with seaweed, sit down, then lie down and finally fall asleep. I wake up to barking, splashing and my face pounding with sunburn. Sound echoes and astounds here as it does when you rise from a dream state; it refracts and shifts like light, like moods.
>
> I look out over the water and see them on a jagged outcropping of rock: a few dark seals, their sleek and impossible bodies—so graceful,

so smooth—slipping in and out of the water. They move from rock to sea and back again, shaking their delicately whiskered faces, water glimmering like sun-touched glass from their whiskers, tails powerful and flapping. Ronan: in Irish, little seal. Ronin: in Hebrew, song. I watch them for a long time, those seals, dipping in and out of the water, cool and calm and singing.

8. First Scenes

The first scene appears at the beginning of the story and bears a great responsibility to introduce your protagonist, her story problems, and her stakes. Incorporating first-scene elements with another scene type at the beginning of the emerging middle helps introduce the unusual world of the middle, the problems that world poses, and the stakes of the outcome in the exotic world. Each genre treats its first scene a little differently, but in all stories the first scene bears the greatest weight of all because it must:

- introduce your compelling protagonist and her emotional position at the beginning of each part of the story.
- orient the reader in the time period and setting.
- show the character grappling with emotional conflict(s) in her shadow world.
- set up a dramatic action goal she'll pursue.
- show how that goal leads to a first, or next, major point of action.
- show her emotional orientation to her ordinary world.
- create a consequence of that action that will need to be addressed by further action.
- use visual and sensory imagery, as well as character reflection and dialogue, to hint at the theme.

This first scene comes from Jonathan Lethem's genre-bending novel, *As She Climbed Across the Table*, which is part love story, part exploration of the meaning of life, and part discussion of the science of the universe. In it, protagonist Phillip's girlfriend, Alice, a physicist at the same university where he is also a scientist, falls in love with a black hole they have manually created in the lab. The premise sounds absurd, but it is remarkably well done. In the following passage, notice how Lethem introduces the characters and setting in just a few short pages, builds a sense of tension through the juxtaposition of the mundane—a man in love going about his day—with the setting of a particle physics lab. After a few pages, you already know that something complicated, even bad, is about to happen.

> I knew my way to Alice. I knew where to find her. I walked across campus that night writing a love plan in my head, a map across her body to follow later, when we were back in our apartment. It wouldn't be long. She was working late hours in the particle accelerator, studying minute bodies, pushing them together in collisions of unusual force and cataloging the results. I knew I'd find her there. I could see the swell of the cyclotron on the scrubby, sun-bleached hill as I walked the path to its tucked-away entrance. I was minutes away.
>
> Unlike the physicists, my workday was over. My department couldn't pretend it was on the verge of something epochal. When the sun set we freed our graduate students to scatter to movie theaters, bowling alleys, pizza parlors. What hurry? We were studying local phenomena, recent affairs. The physicists were studying the beginning, so they rushed to describe or bring about the end.
>
> As I hurtled toward her, carving shortcuts across the grass, violating the grid of concrete walkways, my heart was light. I was in orbit around Alice. I was a fizzy, spinning particle. I wanted to penetrate her field, see myself caught in her science gaze. Her Paradigm Eyes.
>
> The supercollider stretched out, a lazy arm, across the piebald hills above campus. The old cyclotron was like a beehive on top. Underneath, a network of labs was dug into the hill. The complex grew, experiment by costly experiment, an architectural Frankenstein's Monster to crush the human spirit. But as I approached the entrance, double doors of scratched Plexiglas, I felt immune. I knew what lay at the heart of the heartless labyrinth. No immensity was enough to dwarf me.

So I stepped inside. The facility was made of bland slabs of concrete, as if to refute the hyperactive instability of the atomic world. The walls were run through at random with pipes and electric cables, painted gray to match the concrete. The floor thrummed slightly. The facility might have been a giant ventilation system, and I a speck or mote. But I had my target. I walked undaunted.

Alice's wing was empty, though. Alice was gone, and so were her students and colleagues. My footsteps echoing, I wandered the dingy concrete halls, searching the nearby labs. They were empty. Checked the muon-tank observation room. Empty. The computer center. I had never seen the computer center empty, without even a doleful sypersym- metrist poring over high-resolution subatomic events, but it was empty now. I looked in at the beam-control room, but the doors were locked.

I was alone. Just me and the particles.

9. Lay-of-the-Land Scenes

At the beginning of a story, and each time the protagonist passes through powerful Energetic Markers at the middle and the end of the story, you will have a lay-of-the-land scene. Though each lay-of-the-land scene may be slightly different, they will all:

- orient the protagonist in the new physical or emotional location he has entered.
- show the character grappling with emotional conflict(s).
- establish his new or revised goal now that he has passed through the Marker.
- show how that goal leads to a first, or next, major point of action.
- show his emotional orientation as he enters the emerging middle.
- create a consequence of that action that will need to be addressed by further action.
- show differences and similarities between the new and old worlds for thematic significance.
- show that what he notices is most important to him at the time.

The Pulitzer Prize–winning novel *Empire Falls* by Richard Russo begins with a prologue that gives the history of Empire Falls. Following is a partial lay-of-the-land scene that begins chapter one.

The Empire Grill was long and low-slung, with windows that ran its entire length, and since the building next door, a Rexall drugstore, had been condemned and razed, it was now possible to sit at the lunch counter and see straight down Empire Avenue all the way to the old textile mill and its adjacent shirt factory. Both had been abandoned now for the better part of two decades, though their dark, looming shapes at the foot of the avenue's gentle incline continued to draw the eye. Of course, nothing prevented a person from looking up Empire Avenue in the other direction, but Miles Roby, the proprietor of the restaurant—and its eventual owner, he hoped—had long noted that his customers rarely did.

No, their natural preference was to gaze down to where the street both literally and figuratively dead-ended at the mill and factory, the undeniable physical embodiment of the town's past, and it was that magnetic quality of the old, abandoned structures that steeled Miles's resolve to sell the Empire Grill for what little it would bring, just as soon as the restaurant was his.

Just beyond the factory and mill ran the river that long ago had powered them, and Miles often wondered if these old buildings were razed, would the town that had grown up around them be forced to imagine a future? Perhaps not. Nothing but a chain-linked fence had gone up in the place of Rexall, which meant, Miles supposed, that diverting one's attention from the past was not the same as envisioning and embarking on the future. On the other hand, if the past were razed, the slate wiped clean, maybe fewer people would confuse it with the future, and that at least would be something. For as long as the mill and factory remained, Miles feared, many would continue to believe against all reason that a buyer might be found for one or both, and that consequently Empire Falls would be restored to its old economic viability.

What drew Miles Roby's anxious eye down Empire this particular afternoon in early September was not the dark, high-windowed shirt factory where his mother had spent most of her adult working life, or, just beyond it, the larger, brooding presence of the textile mill, but rather his hope that he'd catch a glimpse of his daughter, Tick, when she rounded the corner and began her slow, solitary trek up the avenue. Like most of her high school friends, Tick, a rail-thin sophomore, lugged all her books in a canvas L.L. Bean backpack and had to lean forward, as if into a strong headwind, to balance a weight nearly as great as her own. Oddly, most of the conventions Miles remembered from high school had been subverted. He and his friends had carried their textbooks balanced on their hips listing first to the left, and then shifting the load and listing to the right. They brought home only the books they would need that night, or the ones they remembered needing, leaving the rest crammed in their lockers. Kids today stuffed the entire contents of their lockers into the seam-stretched backpacks and brought it all home, probably, Miles figured, so they wouldn't have to think through what they'd need and what they could do without, thereby avoiding the kind of decisions that might trail consequences.

10. Love Scenes

Stories use relationships to deepen readers' understanding of the protagonist. One of the deepest relationships a character has with another character is an in-love relationship (meaning that the love is intimate and extends beyond, for instance, the love of a mother or father for a child, or the love between best friends, or the love of a character for her pet). A character in love with another involves emotion and thus broadens the reader's understanding of the character as depicted through her body language, dialogue, thoughts, and reactions. Stories come alive through people interacting in meaningful and loving ways. Love scenes:

- show a loving interaction between two characters (or more, as in a love triangle) who have a deep affection for one another.
- show two characters who have a passionate, mutual desire, longing, or deep feeling of sexual attraction, and like each other very much.
- reveal the protagonist's inner self through intimacy with another.

- involve physical, spiritual, and/or emotional passion.
- may or may not involve sex and/or making love.

The following love scene involving sex is taken from the middle of Diana Gabaldon's *Outlander*, which won the Romance Writers of America RITA Award for Best Novel.

The moon was sinking, and I was shivering, half with reaction and half with cold. It was a wonderful feeling to have Jamie lie down and firmly gather me in, next to his large warm body.

"Will they come back, do you think?" I asked, but he shook his head.

"Nay, it was Malcolm Grant and his two boys—it was the oldest I stuck in the leg. They'll be home in their own beds by now," he replied. He stroked my hair and said, in softer tones, "Ye did a braw bit o' work tonight, lass. I was proud of ye."

I rolled over and put my arms about his neck.

"Not as proud as I was. You were wonderful, Jamie. I've never seen anything like that."

He snorted deprecatingly, but I thought he was pleased, nonetheless.

"Only a raid, Sassenach. I've been doing that since I was fourteen. It's only in fun, ye see; it's different when you're up against someone who really means to kill ye."

"Fun," I said, a little faintly. "Yes, quite."

His arms tightened around me, and one of the stroking hands dipped lower, beginning to inch my skirt upward. Clearly the thrill of the fight was being transmuted into a different kind of excitement.

"Jamie! Not here!" I said, squirming away and pushing my skirt down again.

"Are ye tired, Sassenach?" he asked with concern. "Dinna worry, I won't take long." Now both hands were at it, rucking the heavy fabric up in front.

"No!" I replied, all too mindful of the twenty men lying a few feet away. "I'm not tired, it's just—" I gasped as his groping hand found its way between my legs.

"Lord," he said softly. "It's slippery as waterweed."

"Jamie! There are twenty men sleeping right next to us!" I shouted in a whisper.

"They wilna be sleeping long, if you keep talking." He rolled on top of me, pinning me to the rock. His knee wedged between my thighs and began to work gently back and forth. Despite myself, my legs were beginning to loosen. Twenty-seven years of propriety were no match for several hundred thousand years of instinct. While my mind might object to being taken on a bare rock next to several sleeping soldiers, my body plainly considered itself the spoils of war and was eager to complete the formalities of surrender. He kissed me, long and deep, his tongue sweet and restless in my mouth.

"Jamie," I panted. He pushed his kilt out of the way and pressed my hand against him.

"Bloody Christ," I said, impressed despite myself. My sense of propriety slipped another notch.

"Fighting gives ye a terrible kickstand, after. Ye want me, do ye no?" he said, pulling back a little to look at me. It seemed pointless to deny it, what with all the evidence to hand. He was hard as a brass rod against my bared thigh.

"Er … yes … but …"

He took a firm grip on my shoulders with both hands.

"Be quiet, Sassenach," he said with authority. "It isna going to take verra long."

It didn't. I began to climax with the first powerful thrust, in long racking spasms …

11. Recommitment Scenes

Throughout the entire story, the protagonist is often forced to recommit to and re-establish his goals. This is perhaps the first point in the story where the protagonist understands he may need to change in order to survive. Use a recommitment scene at the Rededication Marker and wherever you wish to show your character ready to give up only to find inner strengths and resources to push ahead through his many obstacles. The following occurrences may happen during a recommitment scene:

- The protagonist takes stock of where he is in relationship to his goal.
- He evaluates all that is stacked against him and that stands in his way going forward.
- He assesses himself, asking what he needs to do differently to overcome.
- If the protagonist has been ambivalent about moving forward, he will now fully commit to his goal or create a new goal.
- The protagonist feels confident enough to move forward, though he may worry about what's coming.
- He makes clear to the reader what he plans to do next in pursuit of his goal.
- The plan of action he commits to now often deepens the reader's understanding of the themes of the story.

In the classic and much-beloved *The Secret Garden* by Frances Hodgson Burnett, a recommitment scene hits nearly at the halfway mark through the novel, after the protagonist finally solves the mystery of the crying she hears at night and meets the sickly son of the manor, Colin. A maid comments how the protagonist, Mary, "looked quite a different creature from the child she had seen when she arrived from India. The child looked nicer. 'Tha'rt not high so yeller and tha'rt not high so scrawny. Even tha hair doesn't slamp down on tha' head so flat. It's got some life in it so as it sticks out a bit.'" Mary decides that if "gardens and fresh air had been good for her, perhaps they would be good for Colin." But she quickly finds that her goal of sharing her secret garden with him has problems: As much as "she began to like to be with him, she hadn't known him long enough to be sure he was the kind of boy you could tell a secret to." Then she wavers and turns even more ambivalent about going forward with her goal because Colin hates people to look at him, and she worries he won't like Dickon (Mary's cohort in the secret garden) looking at him.

"Why does it make you angry when you are looked at?" she inquired one day.

"I always hated it," he answered, "even when I was very little. Then when they took me to the seaside and I used to lie in my carriage, everybody used to stare and ladies would stop to talk to my nurse and then they would begin to whisper, and I knew when they were saying I shouldn't live to grow up. Then sometimes the ladies would pat my cheeks and say 'Poor child!' Once when a lady did that I screamed out loud and bit her hand. She was so frightened she ran away."

"She thought you had gone mad like a dog," said Mary, not at all admiringly.

"I don't care what she thought," said Colin, frowning.

"I wonder why you didn't scream and bite me when I came into your room?" said Mary. Then she began to smile slowly.

"I thought you were a ghost or a dream," he said. "You can't bite a ghost or a dream, and if you scream they don't care."

"Would you hate it if—if a boy looked at you?" Mary asked uncertainly.

He lay back on his cushion and paused thoughtfully.

"There's one boy," he said quite slowly, as if he were thinking over every word, "there's one boy I believe I shouldn't mind. It's that boy who knows where the foxes live—Dickon."

"I'm sure you wouldn't mind him," said Mary.

"The birds don't and other animals," he said, still thinking it over, "perhaps that's why I shouldn't. He's a sort of animal-charmer and I am a boy animal."

Then he laughed and she laughed, too: in fact it ended in their both laughing a great deal and finding the idea of a boy animal hiding in his hole very funny indeed.

What Mary felt afterwards was that she need not fear about Dickon.

12. Resolution Scenes

Every story has one major resolution that comes after the Triumph, but along the way are other forms of resolution: between the protagonist and allies when ties have been broken or strained; between people who represent your character's former life and her new one; and even, occasionally, within the protagonist. A resolution scene demonstrates the act of finding an answer or solution to a conflict and resolving a problem in a relationship. Resolution scenes:

- bolster a necessary relationship between the protagonist and an ally.
- deepen ties between characters in a way that will strengthen the protagonist at a key juncture to prepare her for a difficult task.
- bring new allies into the fold.
- occasionally occur in a "false" way between the protagonist and antagonist, where the antagonist uses resolution to manipulate the protagonist into or out of doing something.

In Charles Dickens's *A Tale of Two Cities*, protagonist Sydney Carton meets with an ally, Mr. Lorry, to secure his commitment to Carton's request, which will define the action in the story to come. This resolution scene foreshadows the action Carton plans on taking and launches his ultimate transformation, yet most readers reading the following passage only begin to understand Carton has a difficult task planned for himself that requires the help and support of said ally. The transfer of Carton's certificate to Mr. Lorry sets in place Carton's plan.

> ... Carton was the first to speak:
> "The last chance is gone: it was not much. Yes; he [Dr. Manette] had better be taken to her [Lucie, Dr. Manette's daughter]. But, before you go, will you for a moment, steadily attend to me? Don't ask me why I make the stipulations I am going to make and exact the promise I am going to exact; I have a reason—a good one."
> "I do not doubt it," answered Mr. Lorry. "Say on."

The figure in the chair between them [Mr. Manette] was all the time monotonously rocking itself to and fro, and moaning. They spoke in such a tone as they would have used if they had been watching by a sickbed in the night.

Carton stooped to pick up the coat, which lay almost entangling his feet. As he did so, a small case in which the Doctor was accustomed to carry the list of his day's duties, fell lightly on the floor. Carton took it up, and there was a folded paper in it. "We should look at this?" he said. Mr. Lorry nodded his consent. He opened it, and exclaimed, "Thank GOD!"

"What is it?" asked Mr. Lorry, eagerly.

"A moment! Let me speak of it in its place. First," he put his hand in his coat, and took another paper from it, "that is the certificate which enables me to pass out of this city. Look at it. You see—Sydney Carton, an Englishman?"

Mr. Lorry held it open in his hand, gazing in his earnest face.

"Keep it for me until to-morrow. I shall see him to-morrow, you remember, and I had better not take it into the prison."

"Why not?"

"I don't know. I prefer not to do so. Now, take this paper that Doctor Manette has carried about him. It is a similar certificate, enabling him and his daughter and her child, at any time, to pass the Barrier and the frontier? You see?"

"Yes!"

"Perhaps he obtained it as his last and utmost precaution against evil, yesterday. When is it dated? But no matter; don't stay to look; put it up carefully with mine and your own. Now, observe! I never doubted until within this hour or two, that he had, or could have, such a paper. It is good, until recalled. But it may be soon recalled, and, I have reason to think, will be."

"They are not in danger?"

"They are in great danger. They are in danger of denunciation by Madame Defarge. I know it from her own lips. I have overhead words for that woman's, to-night, which have presented their danger to me in strong colours. I have lost no time, and since then, I have seen the spy.

He confirms me. He knows that a wood-sawyer, living by the prison-wall, is under the control of the Defarges, and has been rehearsed by Madame Defarge as to his having see Her"—he never mentioned Lucie's name—"making signs and signals to prisoners. It is easy to foresee that the pretence will be the common one, a prison plot, and that it will involve her life—and perhaps her child's—and perhaps her father's—for both have been seen with her at that place. Don't look so horrified. You will save them all."

"Heaven grant I may, Carton! But how?"

"I am going to tell you how. I will depend on you, and it could depend on no better man. ..."

13. Transition Scenes

One of the most basic and well-used transition scenes occurs at the First Energetic Marker, Point of No Return. The primary role of a transition scene is to connect the bigger and more energetically relevant scenes. Transition scenes:

- can be short in length.
- establish a logical connection between one scene and another.
- link scenes unlinked by cause and effect.
- clarify and fill in important gaps in readers' understanding.
- give just a snapshot of the protagonist's emotional position.
- guide the reader in the direction you want her to go.
- connect an otherwise episodic presentation of scenes.
- may contain slightly more narrative summary than active scene elements.
- are of less significance than other scenes.
- serve to shift back and forth between subplots and the primary plot.
- fill empty space or a gap between more significant scenes.
- do not have to advance all the essential elements of scene.
- should still nod or point to the theme.

The following transition scene comes from the *New York Times* bestseller *The Language of Flowers* by Vanessa Diffenbaugh. This more narrative transition scene serves to fill a gap between two significant scenes by shifting the reader from the romantic plot developing between the protagonist and her boyfriend, Grant, to a subplot involving a book about flowers that the protagonist is creating, and then back again to a more significant scene that solidifies the relationship between the two characters.

Toward the end of one energetically charged scene, having brought the protagonist to his house to photograph flowers, Grant asks the protagonist if she wants another photography lesson. She says no, and their scene together ends with her waiting "until I saw a light flip on in the third-story window before I turned toward the rose garden."

A transition scene follows.

> In the waning light I photographed the same half-opened white rosebud, writing down in descriptive, nontechnical terms the reading of the light meter and the exact position of the various dials and knobs. I recorded the focus, the position of the sun, and the angle of the shadows. I measured the distance of the camera to the rose in multiples of the length of my palm. When I ran out of light and film, I stopped.

Immediately after she stops, a second energetically charged scene begins.

> Grant was sitting at his kitchen table when I returned. The door was open, and inside was as cold as outside. The sun had disappeared, and with it all warmth. I rubbed my hands together.
>
> "Tea?" he asked, holding out a steaming mug.
>
> I stepped in and closed the door behind me. "Please."

The scene develops, showing them sitting "across from each other at a weathered wood picnic table identical to the one outside," and then taking a tour that significantly advances the intimacy of their relationship.

14. Suspense Scenes

Any scene that creates a sense of uncertainty and insecurity, coupled with apprehension and anxiety, qualifies as a suspense scene. When a reader wants the character to succeed and at the same time fears she will fail, this creates rising tension through suspense. Use suspense scenes to generate excitement and to draw readers emotionally close to your protagonist, keeping in mind these considerations:

- The antagonists are at least as strong as the protagonist and preferably stronger.
- The more unpredictable the antagonists, the greater the suspense.
- The protagonist's emotions should heighten scene by scene.
- The protagonist can worry about an upcoming event to create anticipation.
- Get as close as possible to the character's differing emotions during a conflict. Rather than repeat thoughts and emotions, strive to deepen them.
- The protagonist should begin in, or get caught in the middle of, trouble or danger.
- The emotional, physical, or spiritual stakes for the character should become more complicated during a suspense scene.
- The emotional intensity should increase for the protagonist and not let up until the end.
- The events of the scene or fellow characters should exert pressure on the protagonist to change or act in some way.
- Use dialogue, visual imagery via the setting, and brief internal rumination to reinforce the theme.

This suspense scene comes from Emma Donoghue's novel *Room*. The narrator is a five-year-old boy named Jack who has been born in captivity. His only interaction has been with his mother, who has done her best to teach him about the world beyond their room without making him understand the horror of their situation. He has heard the voice of their captor—his biological father, a man named "Old Nick"—but doesn't know what the man looks like. Unable to stand this life any longer, his mother has concocted a plan to free her son, if nothing else. She fakes the boy's death and wraps him in a rug, and Nick believes he is taking the body to dispose of it, unaware that the boy is alive. Eventually, Nick stops the truck, hearing a sound from the back, and all hell breaks loose. Jack jumps out, is bitten by a dog, and a couple stops to talk with Nick. You don't know as the scene unfolds if Jack is going to be rescued or not, and the agonizing suspense forces you to keep reading.

> Then bam, grabbed from behind, it's Old Nick, his giant hands on my ribs. I messed up, he catched me, *sorry sorry sorry Ma*. He's lifting me up. I scream then, I scream no words even. He's got me under his arm, he's carrying me back to the truck, Ma said I could hit, I could kill him, I hit and hit but I can't reach, it's only me I'm hitting.
>
> "Excuse me," calls the person holding the poo bag. "Hey, mister?" His voice isn't deep, it's softer.
>
> Old Nick turns us around. I'm forgetting to scream.
>
> "I'm so sorry, is your little girl OK?"
>
> "What little girl?"
>
> Old Nick clears his throat, he's still carrying me to the truck, but walking backwards. "Fine."
>
> "Raja's usually really gentle, but she came at him out of nowhere …"
>
> "Just a tantrum," says Old Nick.
>
> "Hey. Wait up, I think her hand's bleeding."
>
> I look at my eaten finger, the blood's making drops.
>
> Then he has picked the baby person up now, he's holding it on his arm and the poo bag in the other hand and he's looking really confused.
>
> Old Nick stands me down, he's got his fingers on my shoulders so they're burning. "It's under control."

15. Twister Scenes

A twister scene reveals a significant twist in the forward movement of the story, often one that comes with a shock or surprise to both protagonist and reader. A twister scene:

- twists the direction of the story away from where previous scenes were leading the reader.
- may reverse your character's fortune or forward progress, and appears to create insurmountable obstacles.
- presents a major turn of events or shock to your character that is neither crisis nor climax but complicates the character's circumstances; in other words, it raises the stakes. The change is detrimental to the character's goals and also reflects his change of emotion.
- reveals character traits and thematic significance foreshadowed and otherwise hidden from the reader until now.

Charlotte's Web by E.B. White has been heralded as the best-selling children's paperback of all time. In the first scene of the book, Fern implores her father not to kill the runt of the pig litter, whom she later names Wilbur. Though saved as a piglet, Wilbur grows bigger and fatter, and the reader and Wilbur both understand that when "the real cold weather sets in" he will be slaughtered and turned into "smoked bacon and ham." While living in the barn, Wilbur befriends Charlotte, a large spider who dwells in the barn's entrance.

In a twister scene in the middle of the book, the action Charlotte takes twists the direction of the story away from where the previous scenes were leading the reader, though in this instance what she does actually twists Wilbur's impending disaster in the direction of hope.

> The next day was foggy. Everything on the farm was dripping wet. The grass looked like a magic carpet. The asparagus patch looked like a silver forest.
>
> On foggy mornings, Charlotte's web was truly a thing of beauty. This morning each thin strand was decorated with dozens of tiny beads of water. The web glistened in the light and made the pattern of loveliness and mystery, like a delicate veil. Even Lurvy, who wasn't particularly interested in beauty, noticed the web when he came with the pig's breakfast. He noted how clearly it showed up and he noted how big and carefully built it was. And then he took another look and he saw

something that made him set his pail down. There in the center of the web, neatly woven in block letters, was a message. It said:

SOME PIG

Lurvy felt weak. He brushed his hand across his eye and stared harder at Charlotte's web.

"I'm seeing things," he whispered. He dropped to his knees and uttered a short prayer. Then, forgetting all about Wilbur's breakfast, he walked back to the house and called Mr. Zuckerman.

"I think you'd better come down to the pigpen," he said.

"What's the trouble?" asked Mr. Zuckerman. "Anything wrong with the pig?"

"N-not exactly," said Lurvy. "Come and see for yourself."

IN SUMMARY

The fifteen scene types allow you to vary the tempo and intensity of your scenes and help determine the amount and quality of information you convey. They are as follows:

1. climax scenes
2. contemplative (or sequel) scenes
3. crisis scenes
4. dialogue scenes
5. epiphany scenes
6. escape scenes
7. final scenes
8. first scenes
9. lay-of-the-land scenes
10. love scenes
11. recommitment scenes
12. resolution scenes
13. transition scenes
14. suspense scenes
15. twister scenes

see p. 1
before continuing

Part One

ACTION

CHAPTER FOUR

ACTION IN THE BEGINNING SCENES

Walking in the Shadows

Scene types addressed: contemplative scenes, dialogue scenes, suspense scenes

Action is the key ingredient, the "on" switch of every scene, and the thing that drives plot. Though we mentioned it in chapter one, just a quick reminder that when we say "action" we mean two things:

1. the action or momentum of people moving physically through space and time, or engaging in dialogue, which creates the sense of "real time" passing and captures a reader's mind and emotions;
2. dramatic action, the action that comprises the events of your plot, where your character pursues external goals in your story in the form of events, and where consequences unfurl.

Without both kinds of action, characters don't come to life and plots stagnate. But the smaller form of action is what lets a reader know you're in scene: characters moving through space and time and conversing with one another.

We will talk about the emotional depths of action in Part Two, but here we'll lay out what kinds of action advance a character toward the "light" of her goals. "Shadow" actions are those actions that keep your protagonist from her goal, including the people and forces that work against her, and her own inner flaws (more on that in the Emotion section). Thus, when her goals are "in the light," they are aligned with her true self and desires—the self she will become when she has reached her goals through dramatic action.

We refer to life in your character's beginning as her "shadow world." This means that your character acts as she does normally in the beginning scenes (though it may not look normal to the reader, especially if you're writing fantasy or science fiction, or if your character leads an unusual life). It's only as pressure from people and events touch upon her own goals and draw her out toward a seam of light, usually at the Point of No Return Energetic Marker, that she begins to see a mysterious (i.e., new, strange, different, exotic) world beckoning her. (Think of a seam of light as a tiny margin, like light peeking from an open door or window.)

Using examples and analysis from a variety of genres of fiction, memoir, and a couple of screenplays, we'll show you how to set up the important tension between the character's goals and the antagonist's interference in the beginning scenes, all viewed through the lens of dramatic action.

ACTION IN THE BEGINNING

Your beginning scenes—or the first quarter of your story and page count—are generally composed of a first scene plus several more scenes whose job it is to introduce your character, the setting and time period, the character's world, and the goal toward which he moves. In other words, this is where you demonstrate all that is *normal to him* at this early stage of his story. But it can't come in the form of dull summary or long, slow interior monologue. Readers are most engaged by characters moving through space and time. In fact, a reader is more likely to suspend her "need to know" instincts if you drop her right in the middle of a compelling or curious action versus trying to explain what's happening or to offer too much setup.

Each genre treats its first scene a little differently, but no matter which genre you're writing in, the first scene bears the greatest weight of all because it must do three important things:

1. set up a complex character with a compelling goal to pursue;
2. show how that goal leads to a first major point of action;
3. create a consequence for that action that will need to be addressed by further action.

After the first scene, the next pivotal scene is one in which your character identifies his external goal and takes a step toward it, by choice or pressure, which will then lead to the First Energetic Marker, the Point of No Return, at the quarter mark of the story. Some craft books refer to this scene as an inciting incident or a hook, but it can also be more subtle, a "call to change" for the character, one that might not always come with the joy of a new adventure but rather the dread of doing something he doesn't want to do.

Genre books such as romance, science fiction, and fantasy tend to jump more directly into the action than literary books, which develop character or setting more slowly and play more carefully with language. Early scenes in a literary novel, such as Ann Patchett's *State of Wonder*, which we'll analyze later in this chapter, may be "quieter" in their action, focusing more on setting the voice and tone of the character, showing the character engaged with his setting, and involving more contemplative scenes or those with compelling dialogue. But the action is still quite present. In other novels, such as Marisha Pessl's *Night Film*, a crime novel, and other mysteries, thrillers, and even romances, the story often starts with more overt action: a murder, a kidnapping, a meeting, an arrest. And in a memoir like Jeannette Walls's *The Glass Castle,* the story is more likely to rely on a combination of action and contemplation as the author weaves her way through ephemeral memories in search of the events that made her who she is.

We Meet a Complex Character
with a Compelling Goal

In order to get readers to accompany the character on her journey, you must present a protagonist the reader can root for. Readers want to either relate to, or cheer for (or both) this protagonist with whom they will spend hundreds of pages. So it's important to write characters who are multifaceted, not one-note "good guys" or other stereotypes. In a nutshell, make sure your protagonist has flaws, and be aware of them at the beginning, because much of her action will stem from her lack of self-awareness.

Not all books open with a big bang, crash, murder, or other intense splash. Your first scene's dramatic action may come a few paragraphs in, or, if you're the type of writer who writes several scenes per chapter, it may even come in the second or third scene.

Your first scene must set up the circumstances that reveal what the action to come will be, or it must show the character engaged directly in an action.

Let's examine the buildup to action in the first scenes of Anne Patchett's literary novel *State of Wonder*. The first scene opens as forty-two-year-old Marina Singh, a research scientist for Vogel Pharmaceuticals (how's that for a complex character—a female scientist working for Big Pharma!), opens a piece of tragic mail.

> The news of Anders Eckman's death came by way of Aerogram, a piece of bright blue airmail paper that served as both the stationery and, when folded over and sealed along the edges, the envelope. Who even knew they still made such things? This single sheet had traveled from Brazil to Minnesota to mark the passing of a man, a breath of tissue so insubstantial that only the stamp seemed to anchor it to this world.

Anders Eckman was part of a research team in the Amazon jungle of Brazil, working with Dr. Annick Swenson on an expensive and first-of-its-kind drug to cure infertility in women—a drug worth billions of potential dollars the company is eager to reap. With Eckman's death, the company has lost their only contact with Dr. Swenson, the head of the drug program, and it can't bear such a loss. Someone will have to go and track her down. Moreover, there's a personal element: Someone has to locate Anders's body and hopefully bring him home to his family.

Readers don't know much about Marina, but we know she is most likely intelligent from this scene. Her attention to the details as she considers how the stamp on the letter "seemed to anchor it to this world" suggests a depth of feeling that makes us want to follow her wherever she goes. Potent tension is introduced with the news this letter delivers, which is about to push Marina into some sort of action. Indeed, the push comes not long after this scene.

The Protagonist's First Goal Leads to a First Major Point of Action

Marina's boss, Mr. Fox—with whom she is also having a clandestine affair—suggests he wants *her* to go to Brazil to track down Dr. Swenson. In fact, Marina had been the board's first choice over Anders for the original trip to the Amazon, but Mr. Fox had fought to keep her at home because of his feelings for her. Marina is understandably overwhelmed and hesitates to take any action. She doesn't want to be forced to make this decision for several complicated reasons. She fears meeting the same fate as Anders. Plus Dr. Swenson had been her mentor in medical school at a time when something terrible had happened in her backstory.

Patchett relies on primarily contemplative scenes in these early pages, mirroring the cocooned nature of Marina's life. This forms a growing feeling of tension and action about to unfold as she mulls over what she should do. Through a combination of contemplation and dialogue, Marina comes to a decision, and thus to an action.

You, too, may choose contemplative scenes in the beginning of your story for some of the following reasons, though be aware that too much contemplation slows action.

Use contemplative beginning scenes:

- in and around action, to build tension and anticipation in the reader.
- to reveal crucial information about the character's internal state of mind and heart before he takes action.
- to create tension between external forces and the character's desires about an upcoming action.
- only minimally—too much contemplation slows action.

Through several contemplative scenes in which Marina remembers conversations with Anders and works out what she should do, the reader grows increasingly uneasy about what will happen next. We know all this contemplation is the precursor to a decision. In essence, a clock is ticking away beneath the surface of Marina's thoughts, whispering, *Will she go?*

> She didn't want to turn back the clock and choose between Anders and herself, to think about which one of them was more expendable in life's greater scheme. She was sure she knew the answer to that one.

Though contemplative scenes at the beginning of a novel generally could slow things down, in this novel they do the opposite by building tension: Marina's thoughts act as an antagonist as she wars with herself over what action to take. We get a sense of a woman who is used to doing things for the greater good and putting others first. It is clear in the passage above that she thinks Anders's life is worth more than her own.

Patchett doesn't allow the pace to get too sluggish, however. She peppers the contemplation with dialogue—keep in mind that well-placed dialogue feels like real-time action to the reader—and uses it to create yet more tension as Mr. Fox puts ever-increasing pressure on Marina to go to the Amazon. He drops tantalizing hints that the research on this drug is further ahead than Marina realized. Possibly the drug exists already. Despite his being her lover and boss, in these early scenes Mr. Fox is also an antagonist, pushing her toward something she doesn't want to do.

"You wouldn't have died." He was utterly clear on this point. "Whatever Anders did, it was careless. He wasn't eaten by a crocodile. He had a fever, he was sick. If you were sick you would have the sense to get on a plane and come home."

Here the external pressure of the antagonist (Mr. Fox, who knows just what to say to lean on Marina) is pitted against Marina's internal pressure (her complex feelings that she *should* go to the Amazon). After all, Dr. Swenson was her mentor in medical school—and Marina knows that meeting up with Dr. Swenson will force her to face the terrible ordeal from that time in her life. Also, Anders was her friend, and Marina is the only other person in the company who does not have a family who relies on her.

But it's not until Anders's widow, Karen, calls her in the middle of the night and asks Marina to go in her stead that Marina commits to the trip. Karen's pressure is not antagonistic; it touches Marina's moral need to do the right thing, acting as a real-world voice that echoes her own conscience. That seals the decision—Marina will go to the Amazon.

This decision leads to a set of next steps: getting her shots, antimalarial drugs, and papers to prepare for international travel. While this may seem innocuous, the antimalarial drugs begin to make Marina feel ill and give her nightmares of her dead father, and thus this seemingly small action in the plot winds up playing a much larger role in her emotional life later in the story. Though we are purposely not discussing emotion in any depth in this chapter so that you can see the bare bones of action, keep in mind that action drives emotion, and emotion affects future action. (More on this in Part Two.)

The Protagonist Is Confronted by Shadow Situations and People Not Under Her Control (Antagonists)

In novels that are more character driven than action oriented, your protagonist is likely to take fewer big actions and instead will experience more contemplation and assessment, or reaction, after events unfold. But in genre books, particularly thrillers and mysteries, there will be quite a few big moments of action where your protagonist has to make a conscious choice to act; in these genres, your character may find herself at several junctures of key action before she even reaches the middle.

In these beginning scenes, when your character arrives at the first key moment of action, she may not yet know what the consequences of pursuing the goal will be, only that she is pulled to act. At this stage she is driven by complex motivations, which will get clearer and stronger in later scenes—and which we'll explore in Part Two.

From here, the antagonists at work against your character become stronger or more numerous. As we said before, Marina's boss/lover is an antagonist who pushes her toward an action she doesn't really want to take. She is also her own antagonist; she puts pressure on herself by feeling that she should—that she must—go to the Amazon on behalf of others (which, we later learn, stems from past actions she took which have left her feeling deeply guilty).

Antagonists can take the form of forces and situations, as well as people. Internal antagonists will also be discussed at length in Part Two.

Showing the Action of Antagonists in Memoir

Antagonists in memoir may be a little harder to pin down, especially if you are writing from the standpoint that everyone in your story did the best they could, or if you are trying not to be judgmental. In this case it may be more helpful to consider the antagonist as the "opposing force" rather than the "villain." Even when there really is a villain in your memoir, it's important not to paint the villain-antagonist as completely evil—humans tend to behave badly out of a complex mix of trauma and tough experiences. You create tension in memoir by showing the contrast of the antagonist's and the protagonist's goals, which drives the dramatic action.

In Jeannette Walls's memoir *The Glass Castle,* her entire world is full of people and situations out of her control; after all, at its beginning, she's only three years old. The dramatic action of her first scene begins, well, quite dramatically.

> I was on fire.

Not only is this an arresting image, we also quickly learn that she is on fire because she tried to cook a hotdog by herself. Her attempt has led to her dress touching the flame of the stove's burner. But it is the way the antagonists in her life—her parents, who are unable to safely care for their children—handle the situation that sets up her future actions. In memoir, you will pay more attention to demonstrating key events in your narrator's life and their consequences than in a fictional plot, since memoir doesn't allow you to create action from raw material.

Jeannette's mother must rely on a neighbor to rush them to the hospital, since her father is out with the car and no one knows when he'll return, a common occurrence.

Despite needing skin grafts and having to endure a high level of pain, Jeannette realizes that life at the hospital is, in its own way, an improvement over home life. It comes with consistent care, food, attention, and perks like chewing gum and clean bedding. In her own three-year-old way, she forms a new goal: to stay in the hospital.

> I also liked it that I had my own room, since in the trailer I shared one with my brother and my sister. … The nurses and doctors always asked how I was feeling and if I was hungry or needed anything.

She befriends the nurses and never complains, for that might prompt her parents to take her home. Her parents, however, for both financial and philosophical reasons, want her released as fast as possible. Weeks before the doctors feel she's ready to go, her father decides he's had enough of these "heads-up-their asses med-school quacks." This is the same man who once took Jeannette's scorpion-stung sister, Lori, to a Navajo witch doctor, and who bandaged her young brother Brian's cracked skull himself rather than admit a second child to the hospital.

After her father fights with her doctor about whether it's okay to release her, he unhooks her from her sling and breaks her out of the hospital, with a nurse screaming and chasing him down the hall. His parting words, meant to sound reassuring, are instead chilling.

> "You don't have to worry anymore, baby," Dad said. "You're safe now."

The reader understands what young Jeannette is also beginning to realize: The very people entrusted with her care are actually dangerous to her health. This tension ripples from the pages throughout the rest of her story.

In these beginning scenes of the memoir, Jeannette's actions are on par with her age and her awareness. She acts only in ways that accord with any three-year-old child's desire to be happy, have fun, feel loved. She isn't old enough or strong enough to leave home or find other supports for herself, though she recognizes when she's in the hospital that it is a safer and more preferable place to be than at home. However, she can't do much about that; she's left to the mercy of her family. Her parents, the antagonists—the opposing force against her—have different goals for her and do whatever they feel is right, whether it's arguing with her doctors, taking the helicopter ride she won in a raffle while she's too sick to go herself, or busting her out of the hospital at the cost of her health and happiness. In fact, the opposing goals of parents and their children is one of the most common sources of action in a memoir.

Fortunately for Jeannette, she is a plucky and determined child—indeed, the forces of her family shape her to be so. Just a couple of days after she has been "rescued" from the hospital, her skin grafts not fully healed, she takes action by getting right back on the stove and cooking herself some more hotdogs.

Her mother has this to say when she catches her barely healed toddler dangerously close to the burners again:

> "Good for you. … You've got to get right back in the saddle. You can't live in fear of something as basic as fire."

Her mother's praise of the hazardous act is as alarming as the father's false promise of safety. This is a world in which Jeannette is clearly not safe, and perhaps one in which a healthy dose of fear would be a good thing. But she is a three-year-old girl with very little say in what happens to her. She does what she must to survive.

Memoirs often rely on dialogue scenes in the beginning because dialogue is what we remember about our lives, and it's a great way to establish the characters of one's real-life story. More important, dialogue feels like action, even if it's not. The energy of people talking creates motion and tension.

Use dialogue scenes in the beginning to:

- create an experience of real-time action.
- reveal action or character.
- reveal plot information without relying on exposition or backstory.

The scene that follows Jeannette's return home and second foray into dangerous cooking is a dialogue scene.

> Dad came home in the middle of the night a few months later and roused us all from bed.
>
> "Time to pull up stakes and leave this shit-hole behind," he hollered.
>
> We had fifteen minutes to gather whatever we needed and pile into the car.
>
> "Is everything okay, Dad?" I asked. "Is someone after us?"
>
> "Don't you worry," Dad said. "You leave that to me. Don't I always take care of you?"

It's a rhetorical question because her parents do not, in fact, always take care of the kids. The memoir's action is comprised largely of how Jeannette learns to rely on her own wits and creative problem solving as her increasingly self-involved, and at times abusive, parents neglect her and her siblings' most basic needs.

The Character Encounters a Seam of Light— an Event, Destination, or Goal—and Actively Moves Toward It by Choice or Pressure

These beginning scenes are all crucial to developing character, but they only launch your protagonist's plot when an incident teases or yanks her out of the shadows of fear or uncertainty and toward the light of her goals and desires. She won't be free of those shadows yet, not by a long shot, but this pivotal turning point in the action provides an opening for her to move through. Here she takes action, by choice or pressure, which will set the story (and thus her life) in a new direction.

Keep in mind that not every character is an ambitious go-getter; more often than not she is pushed toward her goal through pressure or conflict. Her known world may be inadequate to her needs, but it's comfortable and familiar, too. Nobody leaves the familiar without the promise of encountering something better.

In Marisha Pessl's dark crime novel, *Night Film*, protagonist Scott McGrath is a disgraced forty-three-year-old, formerly award-winning journalist, divorced from his socialite wife and shakily co-parenting their precocious five-year-old daughter. His career has been ruined by a story he pursued five years earlier on the famed cult movie director Stanislaus Cordova. Bad things happen to people who work with Cordova, from death to disappearance, and many are too terrified to talk about what happened to them on his sets. Running on hubris and shaky evidence, McGrath gave a bombastic interview on national television, saying Cordova should be "terminated with extreme prejudice."

As his horrified lawyer puts it in plain terms, "You put a hit out on Stanislaus Cordova."

Cordova sued, and McGrath lost his job, his reputation ruined. In the subsequent five years, McGrath has become almost a ghost of his former self; he does not take *any* action.

McGrath's first scene opens with dialogue: He's making small talk at a party of a female friend of his ex-wife, who's taken pity on him since his divorce. Bored out of his mind, he's surprised to get a text message from his old attorney. It says: "Cordova's daughter found dead. Call me."

You might say that the pursuit of justice and the urge to protect the innocent are the clarion calls for McGrath to take action. The unsolved death of an innocent girl, who happens to be Cordova's twenty-four-year-old violin-prodigy daughter, Ashley, awakens McGrath's purpose in life: to seek the truth at the heart of all things.

For the first time in five years, he takes action and cracks open the door of the closet where all of his Cordova files are stored, making a clear choice: Under the premise of finding out what happened to Ashley, he's going after Cordova.

> And unlike five years ago, now I had a lead: Ashley.
>
> There was something violent in the comprehension that this stranger, this wild magician of musical notes, was gone from the world. She was lost now, she'd been silenced—another dead branch on Cordova's warped tree.

But traveling down this road is fraught with potential danger. The Cordova slander suit from years back cost him everything: leads, contacts, and access. And now he's the father of a young child. But McGrath can't rest. He can't stop. He is driven to find out the truth. And since we are in the beginning scenes, Pessl wisely ensures that her protagonist starts this journey basically from scratch. He seeks out the one person who often offers him tidbits of information out of her own steadfast need for justice: a Manhattan homicide cop named Sharon Falcone who worked with him years before. She has as much disgust and loathing for Cordova as McGrath, which makes her a good ally. She meets him on a public bus so she can be sure none of her colleagues see her giving him information.

In this scene, McGrath speaks first.

> "Was it a homicide?"
>
> Sharon shook her head. "No. She was a jumper."
>
> "You're positive?"

> She nodded. "No sign of a struggle. Fingernails clean. She took off her shoes and socks and placed them together at the edge. That kind of methodical preparation, very consistent with suicide …"

McGrath has sharp instincts, and even though Falcone doesn't have any evidence that Ashley's death was a homicide, he now has one more piece of information on which to act: the jump site. He can go to the site of Ashley's death and see if he can scope out any clues.

Pessl brilliantly sets up a story in which each action leads to yet another clear action that McGrath must take. His actions don't lead to instant answers but put him deeper and deeper in jeopardy as he approaches the truth.

One way to think of a story is as a puzzle the protagonist must solve. These may be inner puzzles, such as how to come to terms with abuse, or they might be an unsolved case or a dilemma over how to obtain a lover. Each action a character takes should provide another interlocking piece for the puzzle.

The First Energetic Marker: Point of No Return

Beginning scenes walk your character right up to the lip of a change. It's a passage through a virtual doorway, the Energetic Marker known as the Point of No Return, which will be difficult, ideally impossible, to turn back from once she's entered the middle scenes. Your character's actions here at this powerfully loaded juncture of the story—the end of her time spent in her shadow world—may be some of the first she's taken toward any kind of change in a long time—years, even. Her actions may be badly handled, confused, sloppy, or imperfect, or they may be too methodical, controlled, or cautious. In these early scenes, her actions set her up to step into awareness of herself and over the threshold into the middle, where the beauty and terror of the new, mysterious world will unfold through the largest section of your story.

In *State of Wonder*, the Point of No Return comes the moment Marina tells Anders's wife that she will go to the Amazon to help bring his body home. She can't go back on her word.

For Jeannette Walls in *The Glass Castle*, the Point of No Return is the moment when she chooses to get right back on the stove and face the fire that burned her—a moment of courage and determination that will inform many of the choices she makes throughout her life.

In *Night Film*, the Point of No Return comes when McGrath contacts detective Sharon Falcone. Once he invites another person into his search, and admits aloud that he suspects Cordova of Ashley's death, there is no turning back.

IN SUMMARY

Scenes kick to life through some form of action—particularly the small, moment-by-moment beats that move us through space and time. Beginning scenes also introduce the external plot, or dramatic action, in the first quarter of your story. Comprised of your protagonist's goals opposing those of the antagonist's, action begets action, creating a life of its own, leading the character ever forward into deeper and more complex territory. In the beginning, the action in scenes sets up both the goal toward which the protagonist moves and what, if any, resistance he faces. In other words, beginnings introduce external action that is normal to the character at this early stage of his story. In the beginning scenes:

- establish your protagonist's testing ground and center of conflict.
- set up the tension between what the character wants and what prevents him from his goal.
- show the character meeting and resisting the antagonist's actions.
- give a bird's-eye view of place—not specific details, just an overview to ground the reader.
- emphasize important information the reader needs in order to make sense of the story.

- push into the background all nonimportant information and details the reader does not have to remember.
- remove backstory clutter so the reader isn't confused and is able to move quickly to the heart of the story—the middle.
- show the character pursuing his own external goal, reaching toward a seam of light that leads to inevitable change.

CHAPTER FIVE

ACTION IN THE EMERGING MIDDLE SCENES

Brightening and Recommitting

Scene types addressed: suspense scenes, dialogue scenes, recommitment scenes, lay-of-the-land scenes

In chapter four we covered three scene types that are useful in developing action. First scenes, dialogue scenes, and contemplative scenes help form a promise between you and the reader about your story's pace, the degree of difficulty the protagonist will face from the demands of the action, and the importance of her goals to the world at large.

The First Energetic Marker, the Point of No Return, is a powerfully fraught moment for your protagonist. She has made choices based on the events in the first quarter of her story and now takes a step out of her shadow world. Once she passes through to the exotic world in the middle, there is no turning back.

Action in the middle scenes of a story sets up situations to deepen the reader's understanding of the characters as well as the risks involved in going forward into the unknown world. Scenes at this point in a story are played out in moment-by-moment movement and action, inviting the reader to connect viscerally to the mystery and intensity of the middle.

The middle begins the moment the protagonist crosses into the territory of the antagonists. This is where the real story plays out—it's often referred to as the "good part." In deconstructing the plots and scenes of successful stories, we find that a major task of the middle is to reveal the internal and external shadow side of the characters. That is done by portraying truly perilous action in a mysterious new world.

Consciously highlighting and integrating shadow sides in scenes will create exciting, dynamic plots. You can look for antagonists hiding in the shadows:

- in action where the protagonist is not in control.
- in confrontations and setbacks that force her to confront hidden qualities.
- in settings under the antagonist's rule.
- in turning points that twist the character deeper into unfamiliar territory.
- in imagery that describes these events.

The darker side of a story, the degree of which is foreshadowed in the beginning, now starts, in the middle, to reveal the truth that's been hiding all along in the shadows. An understanding of the dark side of your story helps you create more tension, excitement, and page-turnability. To engage your reader, especially in today's distraction-filled world, you must keep your story exciting. Excitement is created through dramatic action where the reader is never quite sure what's going to happen next and fears the worst for the protagonist.

Scenes that don't have action, emotion, and meaning cause a reader's mind to wander. A reader with a wandering mind detaches from the story and puts the book down. Later, if she does pick it up again, she won't recognize where she left off because, though her eyes skimmed the words the first time, the meaning didn't penetrate.

Because she has to go back to find where she last remembered reading consciously, any true connection to the story has been compromised and the reader may never fully commit to finishing your story.

THE TWO HALVES OF THE MIDDLE

You'll remember from chapter one that the middle is generally divided into two parts, each of which has its own Energetic Marker:

- **THE EMERGING MIDDLE:** Second Energetic Marker, Rededication
- **THE DEEPER MIDDLE:** Third Energetic Marker, Dark Night

The Emerging Middle

The middle begins with the protagonist wary of the differences in this new world in which he finds himself, either cautiously or full-heartedly optimistic about moving forward. It culminates when he is challenged to recommit to his goal. The more the external action caused by his new environment tips him off balance, the more tension and excitement will be present in the scenes. The more determined the antagonists challenging the protagonist, the more tension and excitement in the scenes. The riskier the external action, the more (you guessed it) tension and excitement in the scenes. And the more tension and excitement in moment-by-moment action, the faster the reader turns the pages, eager for what happens next.

The further away the protagonist travels from all he knows, the darker the story turns.

The Deeper Middle

In the deeper middle, the antagonists gain more strength and grow more formidable, and the obstacles and setbacks they concoct make the way to the protagonist's goal riskier and more perilous and challenging. Scenes in the latter half of the middle find the protagonist surrounded by intensifying darkness, which leads to doom and a subsequent crisis. This is where he suffers the Dark Night.

ACTION IN THE EMERGING MIDDLE

The action in the emerging middle is discussed in this chapter, and the deeper middle is examined in chapter six. An understanding of the two parts of the middle shows you how to merge action, emotion, and meaning in a particular order to build energy and excitement.

Of the three key guiding scene layers that explore different aspects of the shadow side of characters' stories—action, emotion, and theme—action creates emotion by forcing the protagonist to face hidden parts of herself, creates overt excitement on the page, and deepens the meaning of the story. The ability to write strong, layered, and engaging action is the key to writing memorable, page-turning plots. You know when you're reading a story with action because the level of excitement pops from the page. The action, and thus excitement, sparks with greater intensity in the middle than in the beginning.

The middle section of stories—the emerging middle and deeper middle—often forms its own plot, with a beginning (as the character enters the middle), a middle that rises in intensity (a major turning point, the Rededication), and an end that rises to peak tension and intensity at the Dark Night.

The First Scenes of the Emerging Middle

One way or another—bravely, awkwardly, or cautiously—the protagonist arrives in the middle, where the story takes off in a new direction and tension builds.

We talked about taking a character on a moment-by-moment trek of transformation, one that is found in all best-selling stories. The real trek begins when the character leaves behind what's familiar and steps into the shadows of the unknown to seize his prize, or so he hopes.

Similar to crafting the first scene of the entire story, the first scene upon entering the mysterious world of the middle bears the weight of grounding, orienting, and preparing the reader for what's coming. For readers to truly appreciate the middle of your story, they must first understand what the protagonist wants now and how the world of the middle operates compared to the world of the beginning.

The Night Circus by Erin Morgenstern, originally published as a young adult fantasy novel, takes place around the development of and happenings in a mysterious wandering circus that opens only from sunset to sunrise. One month after the book's formal release, the novel broadened its readership and crossed into the adult market fantasy romance genre when *The New York Times* described the story as "two love-struck magicians engaged in a battle of imagination and will."

The story centers on the life-or-death competition between the two major protagonists, Celia and Marco, both young magicians performing in the circus. The beginning of *The Night Circus* introduces all the major characters, demonstrates how each of the two contestants train separately to become magicians, and paints a vision of the circus as it becomes a reality. The rules of the competition, which have been purposely obscured in innuendo and vague references, and withheld from Celia and Marco in the beginning of the story, are no clearer in the emerging middle. That Celia and Marco are kept in the shadows reinforces the sense of the unknown and the impending doom of the middle, keeps the two main characters off balance, and forces the reader to turn the pages faster to learn what exactly is happening.

"Part II: Illumination" marks the beginning of the emerging middle section of *The Night Circus*. The first chapter of this section, "Opening Night I: Inception: London, October 13 and 14, 1886," clearly fulfills one of the many duties of a lay-of-the-land scene in the middle by orienting the reader in the time period and setting.

This chapter is divided into a scene and a summary. The scene begins on the grand opening night of the wondrous circus. A nameless, faceless public is delighted and enthralled by the opening ceremonies, as flaming arrows launch in an astonishing array of brilliant colors. These visual details and the sensory imagery hint at themes of timelessness as a fantastical circus clock begins ticking. The presence of arrows in this scene echoes Cupid's arrow; *The Night Circus* is, after all, a love story at its core.

The chapter ends in a summary that winds back time to just before all the splendor and majesty of the opening ceremonies. The wife of the wildcat tamer unexpectedly goes into labor. Hidden discreetly backstage, before the circus opens to the public, she gives birth to twins. Six minutes before midnight Widget is born. Seven minutes after midnight, his sister, Poppet, follows. The birth of Poppet and Widget announces that a change has arrived: The story and the reader move seamlessly into the exotic world of a traveling, magical circus.

Chapter two of the emerging middle, as shown from Marco's point of view, begins after the twins are born. This scene pulls the broad view of the circus nearer to the story and the action through the lens of a major viewpoint character. Marco is in charge of the details of operating the circus, and he knows that Celia is his opponent. While the reader also knows these facts about Marco, they are both hidden from Celia. However, Marco doesn't know whether she knows who he is, which sets up one of the key elements of lay-of-the-land scenes: introducing the protagonist's emotional position at the beginning of the middle as he grapples with emotional conflict(s) in his shadow world.

When Marco discovers that his competition with Celia will take place in the circus, he successfully accomplishes his first short-term goal in the challenge by magically binding himself to the circus with a fire that is intended to never go out. Though he is worried about the scope of the binding, "having never attempted anything on this scale" and "not entirely certain how well it will work," he tosses into his cauldron a "large, leather-bound notebook" intended to tie him to the circus while it travels hundreds of miles away from his location in London. This scene serves to set up his dramatic action goal of winning the competition and shows how that goal leads to consequence after consequence that will need to be addressed by further action.

These two short scenes at the beginning of the emerging middle already give the reader glimpses of the shadow sides of this world, which are hidden from both the public and from the characters themselves.

The Turning Point into New Territory

The antagonists in the middle, combined with the unknown world the protagonist enters, force the character to face that which she fears, avoids, and ignores. This new world is exactly where she needs to be in order to face her dark emotions and feelings. That she does not understand the "rules" of the unknown world (controlled by the antagonists) causes her to fall down, get hurt, make mistakes, hurt others, cause confusion, and lose her confidence.

In the middle of *The Night Circus*, the actions that take place in the new territory of the circus begin to foreshadow the darkness to come. As the story moves deeper into the middle, action moves the protagonist further into the shadow sides of the mysterious new world. A new tent called the Ice Garden magically appears in the circus, and Celia knows it is the work of her opponent. As she circles around trellises covered in pale roses, which, like everything else in the tent, are made of ice, she appreciates how taxing it would be to manage a similar feat, so much so that "she feels fatigued even considering it."

Later, Marco is convinced his opponent is responsible for a new tent, the Wishing Tree, which uses old wishes to ignite new ones. When asked how he can be certain, he replies, "I can feel it. It is like knowing that a storm is coming, the shift in the air around it." The circus grows incrementally darker for both Marco and Celia as the tension intensifies scene by scene.

For faster page-turnability in the lay-of-the-land scenes of the middle, incorporate expectations and elements of suspense in your scenes. Any scene that conjures a sense of uncertainty and insecurity, coupled with apprehension and anxiety, qualifies as a suspense scene. When a reader wants the character to succeed, and at the same time fears she will fail, the result is rising tension through suspense.

The Shadow Side of the Mysterious New Setting Is Revealed, Causing Confusion and Tension

The world the protagonist moves into in the middle is different from what he's used to. It presents:

- a new location.
- a different circumstance.
- a new belief system.
- a shift in mind-set.

The setting serves as an antagonist in the emerging middle as the unfamiliarity and the unknown create an added strain or burden on the protagonist, which in turn causes him to react. The events wearing on him in the middle deepen readers' understanding of him.

In *A Tale of Two Cities*, a classic that has remained in print for more than 150 years, Charles Dickens brings to life an important turning point in world history when the poor and disenfranchised prevailed against the status quo. Dickens does this not only through his incredible gift with words, but also by showing the reader the time period through the action that takes place among the major characters. Through these character relationships, Dickens provides breathtaking action twists.

In the middle of the novel, the reader is immediately thrust into the exotic world of Parisian aristocrats as told from an insider's point of view. This insider is the major antagonist of the story and can be considered a true villain. He remains in the shadows until later in the story, though the initial description of him as "a man of about sixty, handsomely dressed, haughty in manner, and with a face like a fine mask" ends with a warning to the reader: "then, [his eyes] gave a look of treachery, and cruelty." He is the perfect character to deepen the reader's appreciation of eighteenth-century France by demonstrating the contrast between the wealthy class and how "cowed was the condition" of the common people.

By featuring Paris in all its glory as a major setting at the beginning of the emerging middle, Dickens allows us to understand the full extent of the damage and the shattering of the status quo when the city later burns.

In *The Night Circus*, the circus itself is the unknown world. In the beginning, the reader witnesses several characters planning and preparing for the circus. Now, in the emerging middle, we are shown how the circus operates beyond its conceptions as the public is allowed in to experience the fun.

The second scene of the second chapter of the emerging middle pulls the reader nearer to the characters and the action as Celia shows us her point of the view of the circus. This scene qualifies as a dialogue scene in that two characters open up beyond the simple exchange of verbal information to include insight into how the interaction is inwardly affecting them. The scene also points to thematic significance and includes emotional significance of the interaction to the character(s).

Celia has just been "swept up in the somewhat ordered chaos" when the wife of the wildcat tamer unexpectedly goes into labor with twins. She hears "the soft cry that sounds minutes before midnight … ." Then something else immediately follows. She feels it: "the shift that suddenly spreads through the circus like a wave." When she reacts to the shift, the circus contortionist asks if she is all right.

Through their dialogue, we learn that the contortionist is warm and familiar, and believes Celia to be a sensitive person, and that Celia finds both the twins' birth and the lighting ceremony to be remarkable, all of which deepens the reader's understanding of the circus now that it's underway.

The dialogue also serves as a gap in time to slow down and create added significance to Celia's gathering awareness that the competition has officially begun. Beneath the conversation, the reader feels Celia's visceral reactions as she experiences "… an involuntary shiver down her spine, almost knocking her off her feet." She "can only nod," "struggling to catch her breath," as the shiver is "tingling over her skin." Her reactions to the actions taken by her mystery opponent (antagonist) show a spark in her emotions: "… whatever move has just been made, it has rattled her."

Also incorporated into this dialogue scene is the important element of suspense—it sets up Celia to worry about an impending event—which creates anticipation and anxiety in the reader.

The Antagonists Gain Strength

In the middle, the antagonists are at least as strong as the protagonist (and preferably stronger) as well as unpredictable. This is the time in your story to master the art of creating compelling, thematically true antagonists of all sorts—other people, nature, society, machinery, beliefs, and attitudes—to prevent the protagonist from reaching her short-term goals.

Antagonists begin to appear in *The Night Circus* in the form of the other performers and the public. Additionally Celia and Marco serve as antagonists for each other as their developing relationship and feelings intensify, and as their abilities strengthen. Celia's scheming father and Marco's mysterious benefactor both turn darker and more secretive in the middle scenes.

As you write the middle of your story, begin listing the antagonists that appear. Look for people, places, beliefs, nature, and machinery that stand in the way of the protagonist moving forward toward her goal. Explore the worst-case scenarios the antagonists are capable of inflicting on the protagonist to impede her forward progress. Just as the protagonist has her goals, every antagonist has his own set of goals, too. Create conflict in your story by developing goals for your antagonists that directly or indirectly interfere with what the protagonist wants.

The Character Moves Toward a Specific External Goal

Character goals and goal setting are critical for all stories because the protagonist's long-term goal, and the short-term goals he believes will move him closer to the long-term goal, determine the action of a story. Action perceived to be in the service of others creates a deeper bond with readers than action taken simply to achieve a personal desire. The character takes specific action to realize his goal as the antagonists and other characters react, support, and interfere on the way to their goals.

The timing established for the completion of each goal sets the pace of the middle of the story. A ticking clock of necessity, or the threat of suffering punishment or doom propels the story forward. The intensity of the action builds throughout the middle.

Celia's first scene in the emerging middle of *The Night Circus* creates in the reader a sense of uncertainty and insecurity, thus meeting our definition of a suspense scene. Her dialogue scene with the contortionist also communicates the first major point of action in the middle, when she realizes that the start of the circus also signifies the start of the competition. As "she wonders how she is supposed to retaliate," it becomes obvious that she must devise a series of short-term goals to accomplish her long-term goal of winning the competition.

The Character Interacts with New People in New Places and Situations

Stories are all about relationships. Relationships occur between characters, with animals and objects, and also between the protagonist and her personal success or failure.

Secondary characters fill the mysterious world of the middle, and each creates subplots and serves to deepen the reader's understanding of the protagonist, illuminating different aspects of the story's overall meaning.

In the middle of the story, the other characters are either allies who support the protagonist toward her long-term goal, or antagonists. Antagonists control the territory of the middle by either consciously or unconsciously preventing, stalling, or distracting the protagonist from her course of action toward her goal.

Conflict is established when an antagonist in the form of someone else, or something internal or external, interferes with the protagonist's forward movement. The suspense comes from not knowing what's going to happen next and who will win—the protagonist or the antagonist. Tension is a felt response from the heart about what effect the conflict and success or failure will have on both the character's emotional transformation at the overall plot level and her emotions at the scene level.

Lucie, a character in *A Tale of Two Cities*, is a major player in the protagonist's love subplot. Sydney, the protagonist and an Englishman, has determined that Lucie is out of his reach because of his character flaws and her affection for another important secondary character, Charles Darnay, who later becomes her husband. Charles, a Frenchman, drives several subplots, one of which comes directly out of his mysterious backstory and is pivotal to turning the action of the plot.

The Second Energetic Marker: Rededication

Throughout the entire story, the protagonist is forced to recommit to his goal over and over again. Every time he is confronted with action interfering with his progress, his only way forward is to figure out how to successfully fulfill his goal in light of all that has happened in the story so far. Each time he does this and moves forward, he formally rededicates himself to his goal. The scene type often used to convey this is a recommitment scene. The Rededication at the Second Energetic Marker can take place with one specific scene type or with several different kinds of scenes such as a twister, resolution, or epiphany scene.

At the halfway point of every great story, the protagonist takes stock of where he is in relationship to his goal, which reorients the reader in anticipation of the deeper middle and the Energetic Marker of greatest intensity in the entire story so far: the Dark Night.

His evaluation of all that's stacked against him and what stands in his way going forward, as well as his assessment of himself and what he needs to do differently to overcome, is perhaps the first point in the story in which the protagonist understands he may need to change in order to survive.

The halfway mark of the story is the time to reveal what is important moving forward. If the protagonist has been ambivalent about moving forward, now he makes clear his goal, either the same one he had in the first half of the story or an entirely new goal based on what's happened so far. Remember that character goals define the action of the story. Every time the protagonist mentions a goal or recommits to one, the reader better understands the story's direction. Though the protagonist may worry about what's coming, he feels confident enough to move forward.

IN SUMMARY

Action in the middle scenes pulls the protagonist into the exotic world of the antagonists. The middle scenes comprise the largest part of your book; it is twice as long as the beginning or the end. Challenges and conflicts and obstacles interfere with the protagonist's way forward, and she struggles throughout the middle with increasing intensity. When considering action in your emerging middle scenes, be sure that the following statements are true:

- Conflict is central.
- The antagonists grow more powerful, and their goals strengthen and intensify.
- The protagonist's goal and the antagonists' goals grow more in opposition to one another.
- The protagonist's external goal is made clear through actions and words.

- The protagonist resists the antagonist's goals.
- Tension builds to a breaking point.
- The antagonists and the part they play in developing the tension of your character's story are firmly established.
- The scenes deepen the reader's understanding of the antagonist's goals.
- The scenes show all the different ways the character is thwarted from reaching her external goal.
- The scenes show the antagonist's goals intensifying and interfering more directly with the protagonist's forward progress.
- The scenes show the character recommitting to her own external goal, which unwittingly thrusts her toward inevitable disaster.

CHAPTER SIX

ACTION IN THE DEEPER MIDDLE SCENES

Intensifying Darkness

Scene types addressed: first scenes, suspense scenes, revelation scenes

In the last chapter, we covered aspects of the action found in scenes in the emerging middle. The protagonist enters a new world filled with formidable antagonists, and the halfway point of the middle culminates with her challenge to rededicate her time and resources to her goal. Made up of your character's goals, action in the middle begets more action, creating a life of its own, leading the character ever forward. Action keeps the story moving with the help of the resistance she faces.

By the Second Energetic Marker, Rededication, the protagonist has a better grasp of the new world she's been thrust into, either willingly or unwillingly. The rules are becoming clearer as she learns lessons and suffers hardships. She has identified allies and antagonists by their support for or interference with her goal. After she rededicates herself to her journey in one or several scenes and scene types at the halfway point of the story, she enters the deeper middle.

ACTION IN THE DEEPER MIDDLE

The deeper middle is defined by the intensity of the tension between what the character wants and what stands in his way. This intensity rises with each new scene in anticipation of:

- the next action taken.
- the effect the external action causes in the protagonist.
- the protagonist's actions and reactions.
- how that cause and effect contributes to the overall meaning of the story.
- the coming crisis at the Third Energetic Marker, Dark Night.

Similar to the beginning of the book and the beginning of the emerging middle, scenes at the beginning of the deeper middle must incorporate several elements:

- everything the reader needs to know about the protagonist's testing ground and center of conflict in order to make sense of the crisis at the Dark Night.
- tension between what the protagonist wants now and the forces that prevent him from his goal.
- a clear understanding of the antagonist's goals.
- the character meeting with increasing resistance from the antagonists as they interfere with his goals.
- the character pursuing his external goal—reaching toward a seam of light—toward inevitable change.

As the protagonist finds himself firmly in the darkest part of the story, forces that oppose him begin emerging in full force in the form of the setting, nature, society, other people, and so on. These forces can take many forms, including a ticking clock, malfunctioning machines, religion or God, the government, a secret society, vampires, zombies, or aliens. Fraught with cruel antagonists, evil villains, and confusing tricksters, all of whom create dark action, the deeper middle is where the protagonist is also hounded by his own personal shadow, whether this is his fatal flaw or unresolved backstory, which creates dark emotions in him.

As he becomes thoroughly entangled in the dark side of the story, the protagonist finds the antagonists have gained more strength and grown more formidable. The obstacles and setbacks they concoct make the way to his goal riskier and more perilous and challenging. Scenes in the latter half of the middle are filled with action that forces the character deeper and deeper into intensifying darkness, leading to doom and complete failure.

Oblivious to all that awaits him, and having just gained a renewed sense of commitment, the protagonist ventures into the deeper middle by moving steadily toward his goal. Though he knows and understands the new world a lot better now, he still often finds himself confused and uncertain. Just as resolute and as highly motivated as the protagonist, the antagonists follow their own individual goals, which always stand in direct opposition to what the protagonist wants.

We mentioned in the last chapter that middles of stories often form their own plot that begins and ends in the middle. The key difference between the beginning, middle, and end of the entire story and the beginning, middle, and end of the middle section is that, rather than the progression of scenes culminating to show the protagonist at his best (as is the case at the Fourth Energetic Marker, Triumph), the scenes toward the end of the middle rise to peak tension and intensity, showing the character at his worst—at the Third Energetic Marker, Dark Night. The Dark Night casts the protagonist to his knees. It is truly an all-is-lost moment.

Once the protagonist has fully transitioned from the first half of the story into the second half, quieter scenes where the character is in control fall away. Toward the end of the deeper middle, the reader's fear and wonder about what's going to happen next and who is going to win have been steadily growing until finally, just before the end of the middle, action breaks the protagonist.

Antagonists Challenge the Character with Shadow Action

The purpose of the antagonist's world in the middle is not simply to throw roadblocks at the protagonist to knock her from the path and prevent her from obtaining what she thinks she wants. A deeper and more lasting reason for the conflict and challenges in the middle are that they provide the necessary lessons, skills, abilities, knowledge, and beliefs needed for her ultimate success. These are buried in interactions with other characters (relationships).

The middle of *The Fault in Our Stars* by John Green begins when sixteen-year-old cancer patient Hazel Grace Lancaster receives a reply from an assistant to Peter Van Houten, the author of a book she's been obsessed with. The assistant invites her to visit the author if she's ever in Amsterdam.

Hazel and her new boyfriend, cancer patient Augustus Waters ("Gus"), want to obtain a more complete ending to *An Imperial Afflic-tion* by Peter Van Houten. Hazel's obsession runs from the beginning of the novel to the end; solving the mystery of the ambiguous book ending is one of the three main plotlines. (The other two are the romance plot between the two main characters and Hazel's internal plot.)

Solving the mysterious ending of Van Houten's book ties the the-matic elements of the novel together as both cancer patients grapple with life and death, the meaning of their lives, life in general, and "what it means to be human and whether—to borrow a phrase from the angst-encumbered sixteen-year-olds you no doubt revile—*there is a point to it all*," as Hazel says in the book.

When neither teen is willing to accept the assessment they receive from Van Houten via e-mail—that there is no point to his story or to life—the teens use Gus's wish from "The Genies" to travel to Amster-dam and meet the author in person.

At the halfway point of the story, the teens arrive in Amsterdam in time for a romantic dinner, where they recommit to both their relation-ship and to solving the mysterious ending of Van Houten's book. The exotic world of the emerging middle, where Hazel begins a relationship with Gus, becomes even more complicated in the deeper middle, as she navigates her intensifying feelings for Gus in the even more exotic lo-cale of Amsterdam.

Van Houten is a rude and mean drunk who has no intention of giving either Hazel or Gus what they traveled so far to hear. He holds the successful completion of Hazel's goal in his hands and, as a major antagonist, refuses to give her what she wants. In the fight that ensues, as he fires insults at Hazel for her sickness, we learn the real meaning behind Hazel's inquiry. She accepts that the girl in the story, Anna, dies of cancer. But she's desperate to learn "WHAT HAPPENS TO ANNA'S MOTHER?" That her desperation is conveyed in the text of the story in all caps emphasizes how important the answer is to her. We know then that Hazel isn't hoping for relief from her impeding death; she's anxious about what will happen to her parents when she's gone. She wants reassurance that they'll be all right without her.

Active Conflict and Dramatic Tension Twist the Story in New Directions and Show Reversals in Forward Movement

The specific actions the character takes toward realizing his goal comprise the external plot. Conflict and tension make the action in a scene dramatic.

Exciting external action is created when the protagonist's goal challenges the beliefs and abilities he currently possesses. The process of getting from where he is to where he wants to be must be challenging and perilous for the express purpose of testing his determination and burning away old beliefs and behaviors that no longer serve him. He may boldly believe he's up to the task he's set out for himself, only to find how difficult getting to his goal ultimately will prove to be.

In our earlier example, *The Fault in Our Stars*, Hazel's goal for finding a boyfriend is met when she falls in love with Gus. As Hazel moves beyond her day-to-day existence of surviving on the edge of death to actually embracing life and the love of a boy, it forces her to reach and take risks. She must now move from what's easy, or at least familiar, to what's challenging in the unknown world of having a boyfriend. The outcome matters because she wants to experience love before it's too late.

In Amsterdam, after the horrible fight with Van Houten, Hazel and Gus sightsee and go back to the hotel and make love, she for the first time. Soon after, Gus confesses that he is no longer in remission—in the last cancer screening he "lit up like a Christmas tree."

> We arrived in my room, the Kierkegaard. I sat down on the bed expecting him to join me, but he hunkered down in the dusty paisley chair. That chair. How old was it? Fifty years?
>
> I felt the ball in the base of my throat hardening as I watched him pull a cigarette from his pack and stick it between his lips. He leaned back and sighed. "Just before you went into the ICU, I started to feel this ache in my hip."
>
> "No," I said. Panic rolled in, pulled me under.

This revelation scene reveals a significant twist in the forward movement of the story. Readers expect Hazel to die, but instead she is presented with a major reversal. The twist that Gus is no longer in remission, that he very well could die first, is detrimental to their mutual goal for a long-term relationship and reflects a dramatic shift in the emotions of both characters.

The Shadow Pursues the Character and Thwarts Her Actions

Death, which has pursued Hazel throughout her fight with cancer, is the major antagonist of *The Fault in Our Stars*. Now, toward the end of the middle, it comes for Gus instead. Hazel finds Gus sitting in his car in a parking lot on his way to buy cigarettes. His G-tube is infected, and he is covered in his own vomit. Desperate and humiliated, Gus barely hears Hazel when she tells him she loves him. He continues to decline as Hazel demands he make promises for the future, continuing to believe he'll live.

> "You're okay," I told him. I could hear the sirens.
>
> "Okay," he said. He was losing consciousness.

"Gus, you have to promise not to try this again. I'll get you cigarettes, okay?" He looked at me. His eyes swam in their sockets. "You have to promise."

Action at the Dark Night

The Dark Night Energetic Marker is explained in chapter one of this book as the place of explosive and devastating dramatic action and the destruction of the old world order. The character's belief system has been shattered, his confidence ravaged, all forward momentum destroyed. The Dark Night is the moment of highest dramatic action in the story and the lowest point of your protagonist's journey, a time of crisis, loss, even death (whether a literal death or the stripping away of illusion). After this moment of destruction, he cannot return to his shadow life or to his old ways. The Dark Night serves as a wake-up call that changes his emotional development and will affect the dramatic action of the rest of the plot.

We recommend you use some of the following scene types at the Dark Night Marker:

- crisis scenes
- twister scenes
- suspense scenes
- dialogue scenes
- epiphany scenes

At nearly the end of the middle of *The Fault in Our Stars*, readers no longer see, nor are conscious of, all the steps Hazel takes to coordinate the tubes for the oxygen tank she wheels behind her. We hear little of the rituals that keep her alive, having already grown quite familiar with them earlier in the story. She has changed, grown, matured, and transformed, and we see it first in her competence and independence in her Dark Night scene as the man she loves lies dying in his car in the parking lot.

However, to gain her independence, first Hazel must give up something that no longer serves her. Always dependent on her parents, Hazel suffers guilt for being their primary reason for living. Now that Hazel has changed, her relationship with her parents must shift to accommodate her growing independence.

The Dark Night plays out over one or more scenes and scene types. At this point in the story, just as the protagonist believes he's about to achieve his goal, the antagonist wins and the protagonist loses everything. Now at his worst, with his emotions at their most extreme, the protagonist comes to the darkest moment in the entire story, which is shown through action.

The Dark Night of *A Tale of Two Cities* is at exactly the three-quarter mark. Lucie has married Darnay in London, and together they start a family of two young children as the revolutionaries in France release political prisoners to gain power. When Darnay learns of the peril of his good friends and the woman he loves, he determines he must travel to France to more completely separate himself from "the bad deeds and bad reputation of the old family house." Once there, Darnay is arrested. When he is arrested for the second time as a prisoner of the Republic, his father-in-law Doctor Manette, who was influential in having him released the first time, is powerless to get him released this time, having been stripped of all his influence. At this point, Carton, the protagonist, takes center stage in the story and consciously begins the profound transformation he had unconsciously been undergoing since his recommitment scene at the halfway point in the novel.

At the Third Energetic Marker of *Winter's Bone,* the award-winning screenplay written by Debra Granik and Anne Rosellini, based on the novel of the same name by Daniel Woodrell, seventeen-year-old Ree takes a drastic step. She tries to save the house where she, her ill mother, and two young siblings live. In her attempt to meet with the man she believes knows the location of her missing father, she is beaten nearly to death.

Energy Wanes

The Dark Night, the highest point in the story so far, qualifies as an Energetic Marker because what happens in this scene or scenes shifts and turns the energy of the story in an entirely new direction.

Immediately after the Dark Night, your protagonist crashes, and the energy of your story begins a downward procession. The action scene(s) that follow will contain a marked change in energy—a lull in the urgency that comes immediately after the most major conflict in the story so far. The pace of the story slows after the Dark Night, allowing your protagonist to fully integrate what has gone wrong.

The scene or scenes immediately following the Dark Night do not qualify as an Energetic Marker. Though they are fraught with emotion as the protagonist reels from what just happened, more emphasis is put on reflection, experiencing epiphanies, and possibly mourning over loss.

No matter how despondent, destroyed, or discouraged your character is after the Dark Night, she must pick herself up yet again and begin to consider what to do next in the aftermath of the dark action. She'll also take into account all she has learned throughout the entire middle of the story. She formulates a plan to take her to what she believes will be her ultimate triumph. Often, before the protagonist can move beyond her breakdown to find a breakthrough, she must first come to an understanding of what went wrong.

The time after the Dark Night and before the protagonist travels into the end of the story can differ greatly depending on the character's traits. If the character is more internally driven, she may put off acting and spend more time doing the following:

- slowing down.
- reflecting upon how she is doing.
- evaluating the behavior and reactions that contributed to her downfall.
- looking at what went wrong from all angles.
- learning from her mistakes.

If, however, the protagonist is more spontaneous and impulsive, she may spend less time in reflection and introspection, and instead spring into action without pausing to evaluate what went wrong. She may:

- think less.
- act faster.
- multitask.
- focus less on herself and her responsibility for her downfall to concentrate primarily on achieving the goal.

Those characters that do slow down in the waning action may show their inner thoughts more deeply in an epiphany scene. As explained in chapter three, an epiphany is when something breaks open in the heart and mind of the character, allowing her to realize her part in her own failures and forcing her into a new understanding of herself. Often the Dark Night forces an ensuing epiphany scene where the character begins to grasp her dark or weak side, and assesses what changes need to be made on her part. Because epiphany scenes carry more emotional weight than action scenes do, the forward movement of the story slows. Depending on how long it takes for your character to truly get out of her own way and reach victory, a series of epiphany scenes may be necessary.

In ensuing epiphany scene(s) after Dark Night scene(s), the character gains surprising new insights into the action happening around her, "awakens" to element(s) and clues she's been oblivious to, and/or breaks through denial about the reality of the situation. This new understanding should be revealed in a very clear way and will directly affect choices and decisions she makes as she moves forward.

After grasping where she is now in the dark action, she lets go of what no longer serves her and assembles all the necessary equipment, allies, beliefs, and knowledge necessary to give her a fighting chance at the Fourth Energetic Marker, Triumph. She can now cross into the end of the story, where she begins her final ascent.

In the aftermath of the Dark Night of *Winter's Bone*, Ree's uncle Teardrop comes to take her home, putting himself in grave danger. She is covered in blood and barely able to walk on her own. In the truck, before helping her into her house, Teardrop finally reveals the secret that

Ree must know and understand in order to devise a plan to accomplish her long-term goal.

Often, character goals change in a story based on the dramatic action. However, Ree's long-term goal stays the same throughout the entire movie and book. Though her actions are what get her beaten up, her attempt to gain access to the kingpin of the region and then negotiate for help were simply short-term goals she set for herself. They were yet another step forward in gaining access to her long-term goal of securing the house for her family.

Teardrop tells her what he knows and what he doesn't know. He also warns Ree of the danger she is in as she drifts in and out of consciousness. Because she must regain her strength in order to take on the action needed at the end of the story, this downward slide accounts for several short scenes, each of which assists her in coming up with her final plan of attack.

The Search for Meaning

Though this book concentrates primarily on themes and meanings in stories in the last section of this book, the deeper middle is a good place to begin thinking about the theme of your story. Usually the theme and meaning emerge from the dramatic action and the overall conflict of the work. What or who is creating the primary conflict? Where does the conflict stem from, and what questions does this conflict give rise to? As you consider these questions, jot down the ideas that come to you and save them for when you get to the final section of this book.

For example, in *A Tale of Two Cities*, the protagonist (who will be described in more detail in the emotion section of the middle) is a deeply flawed and wounded man. The greatest conflict and dramatic question of this novel is whether he will overcome his flaws to transform himself to the level capable of ascending to the role of a hero, or if he will descend more deeply and drink himself to death.

IN SUMMARY

Action in deeper middle scenes rises in energy and tension and conflict, entangling the protagonist in the dark side of the story, where antagonists are stronger and more formidable, and obstacles and setbacks are riskier, more perilous, and more challenging than anywhere else in the story so far.

When writing the action in deeper middle scenes, keep the following in mind:

- Antagonists always represent shadow characters creating shadow action, which challenges the character.
- Active conflict and dramatic tension twist the story in new directions and show reversals in forward movement.
- The dark action in the middle affects the goals the protagonist sets for herself.
- The shadow pursues the character and thwarts the protagonist's actions.
- The protagonist is surrounded in intensifying darkness leading to doom.
- Dark action moves the protagonist to her ultimate breakdown and crisis.
- At the Third Energetic Marker, action out of the character's control causes her to fail.
- The energy of the story and dramatic action wane after the Dark Night.
- Different characters act and react differently to the dramatic action at the Third Energetic Marker.
- Themes and meaning may rise from the dark action and conflict in the middle of the story.

CHAPTER SEVEN

ACTION IN THE END SCENES

Seeing the Light

Scene types addressed: epiphany scenes, transition scenes, crisis scenes, suspense scenes, triumph scenes, resolution scenes

Just like beginning scenes, end scenes are powerfully charged stages of a character's story. The end scenes of your book comprise the final quarter of your story and page count. But don't be fooled—quite a lot of action still needs to take place. As your character emerges from the tangled and intense shadows of the action in the middle of the story, she is vastly changed, and many things have been stripped away, bringing both loss and clarity.

ACTION IN THE END

While the protagonist has suffered as a result of the dramatic action of the middle, it has all been for a purpose; he now has a much clearer idea of the actions he must take to realize his goals. Now that some obstacles are out of his way or behind him, he also has the capacity to create new goals that better align with who he has become and the choices he has made. Now he's headed toward some of the most intense and dramatic action of your entire book: the Triumph Energetic Marker, the most potent climax scene in your story.

Transitioning from Deeper Middle Scenes to End Scenes

The middle was the proving ground for your character. In the beginning scenes, many of your character's actions derived from her flaws, her lack of awareness about herself, and the challenges ahead (and even, possibly, behind her), but this is no longer the case as she leaves the middle and builds toward the climax. At the end you have a character who knows herself, knows what she wants, and knows what she has to do to get there. She is no longer a victim of circumstance, and her actions will demonstrate she has integrated the shadow lessons she has learned.

When we last discussed Marina Singh in *State of Wonder*, she was still in the beginning scenes and had just taken the terrifying action of traveling to the Amazon and hopefully connecting with the mysterious Dr. Annick Swenson, head of the project her pharmaceutical company had been working on. Marina's secondary goal was to shepherd home the dead body of her friend and colleague, Anders. She did not look forward to going, but her sense of obligation won out. Marina's decision was also emotional, as it involved a very difficult past event from her life. While we won't discuss that past event in this chapter, it is a reminder that action sets up the circumstances for emotion to unfold.

Much happens to Marina in the territory of the middle. When she finally meets up with Dr. Swenson, the elderly doctor is cold and aloof, reawakening Marina's old demons, particularly her fear that Dr. Swenson despises her. Every step of the way, Marina doubts that she has made the right choice and wonders if she has the courage to take her next action.

However, like any protagonist worth her mettle, Marina finds courage at each step to do what she must. Without courage, your characters can't proceed to the next step. And courage, in many cases, is at first faked but then becomes real as the character proves to herself that she is capable.

When she journeys with Dr. Swenson to the Amazon, to the remote Lakashi village where Dr. Swenson has been doing her covert work researching a fertility drug, and where Anders himself was last seen alive, Marina knows her actions carry grave weight, not only for her future with her employing company, Vogel Pharmaceuticals, but also for her lover and boss, Mr. Fox, and for Anders's wife and children, who want closure.

Marina's crisis at the Dark Night Energetic Marker—her greatest moment of loss—comes in two parts: in rescuing Easter, a beloved Lakashi boy she has bonded with, from the grips of a deadly anaconda, and in performing a potentially fatal surgery on Dr. Swenson after Marina learns the shocking truth (no spoilers here!) about what Dr. Swenson has actually been doing in the jungle.

This two-part crisis cracks open the formerly timid Marina and creates a woman ready to take the action necessary to track down Anders's body so she can return home and bring closure to all. The crises bring us to the beginning of the end of her story.

Keep these things in mind during transition scenes from middle to end:

- Your protagonist takes action with courage and confidence.
- Your protagonist knows what she must do next, even if she doesn't know exactly how to do it.
- The stakes are rising to a fever pitch of intensity as your protagonist engages in more action and less contemplation.
- The protagonist will not turn back on her chosen action now, no matter how difficult.

No Turning Back: Crossing from the Deeper Middle into the Light of the End Scenes

After the Dark Night, your character crosses out of the exhausting and clarifying intensity of the middle and into the highly charged territory of the end. It is another juncture in which your protagonist can't retreat—otherwise his journey will have been in vain, and your reader will be ticked off! At this stage your character moves toward the light of personal integration in his actions, leaving behind his damaged, broken, or troubled self in one form or another and acting with inner strength, outer courage, and powerful decisiveness. Whatever goals he set for himself at the beginning are now much more in reach, or else he has reassessed them and set new ones with recently gained knowledge to bolster him.

At this stage of the story, you will most likely employ suspense, epiphany, or twister scenes. There will be more action than contemplation or time for focused emotional process.

Epiphany End Scenes

Epiphanies are powerful, sometimes painful, and often relieving moments of clarity for your protagonist. Though your character learns something about herself and others in these types of scenes, they can still be fast, intense, and full of action. Just because a character has an epiphany does not mean she has time to luxuriate in her feelings—that can come later in a contemplative or resolution scene.

In Jeannette Walls's memoir *The Glass Castle*, the epiphany scene, before the Triumph Energetic Marker, is signified by her first and, as she declares, "last," whipping from her father. Already a teenager who has survived—along with her three siblings—neglect, poverty, starvation, their father's drunken rants, their mother's bipolar highs and lows, and moving more times than she can count, Jeannette gains sharp, painful clarity about her mother's treatment of her and her siblings. She takes action and speaks her truth.

> "If you want to be treated like a mother," I said, "you should act like one."

In response, Jeannette's mother erupts and threatens to sic Jeannette's father on her when he gets home. Jeannette does not take the threat seriously, so she is shocked when her father makes good on it.

> Dad seemed to be waiting for me to drop my eyes, to apologize and tell him I was wrong so we could go back to being like we were, but I kept holding his gaze. Finally, to call his bluff, I turned around, bent over slightly, and rested my hands on my knees.
>
> I expected him to turn and walk away, but there were six stinging blows on the backs of my thighs, each accompanied by a whistle of air.

The whipping is injury added to insult, and it expands Jeannette's epiphany to include the understanding that she does not have to be a passive victim; she can choose not to take this abuse any longer.

As is common in the quieter form of memoir, where you can't always create perfect action out of the facts, Jeannette's epiphany empowers her to make a decision that is tantamount to an action even though it takes the form of a quiet decision.

> … like Lori, I was going to get out of Welch. The sooner, the better. Before I finished high school if I could. I had no idea where I would go, but I did know I was going.

The Protagonist Makes New Plans for Herself Based on the Integration of Shadow

Following the crossing from middle to end scenes, you should have one to four scenes that focus on tense, tight action and swift pacing as you build toward the Triumph. These are preparation scenes in which your character gathers forces, momentum, knowledge, and courage to do what must be done. He may spend time arming the troops before the war, securing the homestead before the storm, or bracing for an oncoming confession. Here your protagonist may rally new and old allies, mend fences with minor antagonists to bring them into the fold, and put aside smaller needs or goals to make himself available for the larger action about to take place.

Here there is no more equivocation. Your protagonist will not go backwards, will not back out, will not give in to any fear. Here, he will act from a place of integration—he has learned the hard way, has suffered losses at the hands of antagonists and his own flaws, and is a sharp, well-honed, purposeful presence ready to do what must be done. There might even be a moment of awareness for your protagonist within this rallying of new strength, in the form of a thought or a dialogue exchange with another character, that points to just how different he is from where he started. Something to the effect of: "You never could have done this if you hadn't suffered X along the way."

Crisis End Scenes

Though the biggest moment of crisis occurs at the Third Energetic Marker, Dark Night, your character will also experience smaller crises in the end scenes, in which she will grapple with a difficult or seemingly impossible choice or action that will change the direction of her story. In *State of Wonder*, we begin the approach to the Triumph with Marina in crisis. She learns that the deceased Anders has possibly been seen in the neighboring village of the Hummocca people. The Hummocca, unlike the Lakashi, are not known for their kindness to foreigners; in fact they are often downright violent. So, a newly strengthened Marina makes an informed decision to risk her life in a rescue mission. After all, finding out what happened to Anders—and bringing him home, dead or alive—is the primary action goal of the story, the one that sets her on the path in the first place.

Learning that Anders is alive is a serious moment of crisis for Marina; she is just about to go home and admit her losses, the biggest being that she could not find Anders's body. She has been cracked open by truths and experiences far beyond her original understanding, and some of her oldest wounds have been healed. However, if Anders is alive, this changes everything. She must go and get him. (This turn of events also has emotional implications for her character, considering that she risked her life to travel to the Amazon because she believed that he was dead.)

In the end scenes, crises arise to motivate your protagonist to positive action and to prove to herself and others that she possesses newly acquired skills and inner steel. These crises in the end scenes reveal that your character is no longer weak or waffling—which manifests in the kind of action she takes.

Formerly timid, Marina now demonstrates that she can survive, even surmount, a crisis.

> "I should go now."
>
> "After we've thought it through," Dr. Swenson said. "First there has to be a plan."
>
> Marina shook her head, thinking of Karen Eckman and what she had said about Anders not being comfortable with the trees. ... "I don't think tomorrow's going to be any better." And with that she left, Easter trailing behind her.

Zoom in on the scene where your character crosses from the middle to the end—it should be an unforgettable moment of conscious action in which the character's final story goal is in sight.

In *The Glass Castle*, this crossing-over scene is subtle but memorable. After Jeannette decides to no longer take her parents' abuse, she encourages her artistic older sister, Lori, to apply to New York art colleges, and plans on going with her. She is done waiting. She buys a pink plastic piggy bank and deposits the $75 she has earned at her after-school job. In narrative, she declares: "It would be the beginning of my escape fund."

The Character Engages in Actions Toward a Specific Goal That Reflects an Integrated Self, and Intensity Increases

Once your character crosses from the middle to the end scenes, intensity increases in massive proportion, and all actions reflect a character who is integrated and stronger. You'll rely on greater suspense here (you may also find strong use for dialogue and twister scenes).

Suspense End Scenes

The suspense scene is a writer's best friend, especially when writing action, and it's the scene type you'll probably use most often. Its hallmarks of uncertainty and apprehension build crucial energy at the end, when you want to ratchet up the intensity. The greater the stakes and the bigger the risks, the more rapt your reader will be.

In *Night Film*, at the beginning of the end, fallen journalist McGrath has been through a journey to hell and back and has taken a good, painful look at himself. In his single-minded pursuit to prove the guilt of cult director Stanislaus Cordova for the death of Ashley, Cordova's daughter, McGrath sees a reflection of himself and his own driven nature in Cordova's films. He has, in effect, become one of the protagonists of Cordova's movies—a man who, in the course of a perilous journey, comes to hard truths about himself by undertaking dangerous and risky actions in pursuit of an idea or notion.

Suspense remains high in the actions that unfold. By the end of the middle, McGrath has lost custody of his daughter, who was injured during his pursuit of Cordova and has fallen into a coma. He is deep in a thicket of newly sprung clues that point toward answers, creating palpable uncertainty at every turn. Aware at last that his choices and obsession have caused near ruin in his life not once but twice, he finally attempts to put things right, shifting the direction of his plot.

Though tempted to give up after dozens of dead-ends, McGrath realizes that he must finish what he started, and the only way to get answers about Cordova is to go to The Peak, the mansion where Cordova lived and filmed most of his movies, a place that all of McGrath's sources cite as the locus of Cordova's terrible deeds. It's also a place that taps into McGrath's deepest fears.

The moment McGrath, along with his sidekicks, Nora and Hopper, crosses from the middle to the end is when he decides to embark upon The Peak. This is clearly demarcated as a moment of great potential action and also potential failure.

> The plan was a blind risk—not to mention illegal, immoral, crossing the line of even the slackest ethics of investigative reporting, totally outrageous. It could very well get one of us arrested—or injured. For me, it could mean a new low of professional disgrace. ...
>
> "Okay, troops. Let's go over this one last time."
>
> I unzipped the backpack, removed the map.
>
> Our carefully hatched plan—it was the rope for us to hold on to.

The characters are full of conflict about what they'll find at The Peak, but they are driven to seek answers that have eluded them, and so they go, despite the dangers. Pessl does not hold back on the suspense, taking McGrath through a series of increasingly unsettling and mysterious events—uncovering horrors, clues, bizarre characters who reveal more to McGrath than he could ever have expected, accidents, hallucinations, and more. The reader is kept completely on his toes throughout the scenes that follow, straight through to the disturbing and nearly tragic Triumph.

Regardless of the type of scene you use after the Dark Night to show your character's transition to the final quarter of your story, by the time your character crosses from middle to end, there should be no more doubt about what she has to do and what the stakes are. She may still have to rally some last-minute courage or allies, and the opposing pressure from the antagonist will be at an all-time high. Waffling and indecisiveness are reserved for beginning and middle scenes. In the end, you want to take your newly courageous, strengthened, or determined character and drive the stakes even higher by increasing the tension and danger in the final scenes.

The Antagonist's Pressure in the End Scenes Drives the Stakes Ever Higher

From this point forward, the intensity and stakes of the remaining scenes rise to a crescendo as your protagonist prepares to complete the story goal he either set out to achieve or that he has realized is his true goal. The antagonist will be at full power here, working against your protagonist like never before. Your protagonist is moving toward the highest point of dramatic action, the Triumph, during which he will face off with his antagonist and the remnants of his weaker self for the last time.

Every character has a different set of goals. In a quieter literary novel, the action of the Triumph may be as simple as showing up at the right place and time to reveal a necessary truth. In other genres, it may be the moment the troops prepare for battle or a law enforcement agent goes in for the rescue.

At this juncture in *State of Wonder*, Marina is much changed from the timid person we met in the beginning; she has been emboldened to do what is right no matter the risk. She acts with courage and determination. Once afraid of getting on the rickety boat, she now hops on. She is accompanied by only one man for assistance plus the orphan boy, Easter; she departs before anyone else joins her, because she wants to be responsible for as few lives as possible. She also wants to get in and out as fast as she can.

Patchett doesn't disappoint, piling on the intensity and danger. The antagonists—in this case the Hummocca tribe—are ready for battle. As soon as the boat nears the Hummocca tribe's territory, Marina finds herself and her companions in an extremely perilous situation.

> And that was when the arrows came raining down on either side of them, half of them making sharp clicks as they hit the deck while the others parted the water like knife blades and slipped inside.

The arrows don't wound anyone, but they *are* meant to intimidate, and a mortal threat is contained within the gesture. Still, Marina refuses to turn back; she steers the boat to the shore, where the tribal Hummocca people run down to face off with her. With them is a white man. As Marina assesses whether this is Anders, the Hummocca spot Easter—the orphaned boy whom Marina has always thought was Lakashi. But it soon becomes clear that he is actually of their tribe, and they want him back.

Caught between her loyalties, Marina only hesitates for a moment. She remembers her original deal to return Anders to his family and does what she must, taking Anders away before they are all killed.

To keep the stakes high as you approach the Triumph, make sure your character acts accordingly:

- He doesn't hesitate or halt but moves steadily forward.
- He meets obstacles with strength and takes empowered and courageous actions.
- He does what must be done, even if it comes with a cost, and saves reflections and emotions for later.
- He will no longer let the fear of his antagonist(s) keep him from taking action.
- He may still have to pay a "price," be it a battle scar or a haunting reminder of what he fought for, though he ultimately emerges victorious.

The Fourth Energetic Marker: Triumph

At last, your character has struggled and changed, stepped further beyond the shadow and her comfort zone than ever before, and found new resources and inner strength she didn't know she possessed. She has been laid low and come back from it, and is almost fully integrated into this new person as she approaches the last, final, major confrontation, the climax.

The Triumph:

- is the high point of dramatic action (whether quiet action, as in memoirs, or epic action, as in fantasy journeys).
- is the final clash of the antagonist and protagonist.
- shows the protagonist's actions as sure and courageous—wounds and fears are fully integrated and surmountable.
- is a victory for the protagonist over her obstacles and the antagonist.

- is the culmination, the last battle or final confrontation, of the protagonist's larger story goal(s).

Marina's Triumph has arrived, and she must act wisely and carefully: If she keeps Easter, they will all be killed, and the child will be taken anyway; if she brings Anders back, as she set out to do at the beginning, they will live, but Easter will be left behind, betrayed and terrified. It is a victory with a steep cost. Marina has grown strong and courageous enough at this stage of the story to make good on her original goal—to bring Anders home—and accept that Easter's fate is out of her control. She faces her destiny with courage and saves Anders.

In *The Glass Castle*, once Jeannette has decided she is leaving town with Lori, she acts with focus. The Triumph at first looks like defeat: Their father ruins a sculpture that Lori has made for her application to art school, and Lori, depressed and discouraged, abandons her plans to go. Then the sisters discover that their piggy-bank savings have been stolen by their unapologetic father.

> "I'll never get out of here," Lori kept saying. "I'll never get out of here."
> "You will," I said. "I swear it." I believed she would. Because I knew that if Lori never got out of Welch, neither would I.

Jeannette refuses to let this be the end of her plan for escape. She has changed from the child at the mercy of her parents' actions and no longer relies on them. She vows to do whatever it takes to improve her and her sister's life.

When the family she babysits for tells her they are moving back to Iowa and offers to take her with them for the summer, she asks if, instead, they'll buy Lori a ticket to New York. She knows that the only surefire way she can get herself to New York is if Lori goes first. It works. She gets Lori out of town and secures her victory over her father.

In memoirs, the Triumph scene may take the form of several small scenes; unlike fiction, where you can tailor the Triumph to your exact needs, you may instead have to show the way antagonists—comprised of forces, people, actions, and decisions—all come together to lead your character into the light of change or victory.

In memoir, the antagonist may even be something within the narrator herself that she overcomes, such as drug addiction, mental illness, or low self-esteem.

Resolution Scenes: The Character, Transformed, Takes Action in Her New World

Though it often seems as though the story is complete after the Triumph, there is usually one, and possibly two or more, short scenes that conclude the story and complete the resolution. When possible, it's nice to build a parallel between your first and final scenes to echo elements that have now been integrated into your character. You can demonstrate this contrast in his actions. A protagonist who was passive or timid at the beginning can now be shown making a confident choice. Characters are held back and weakened by the wounds of their pasts at the beginning. By the final scenes, they have overcome these weaknesses and behave as healthy, whole individuals. Often a character may return to the shadow world he emerged from in the first scenes, even if only to visit, as a way of showing how he is no longer the same person he was.

Resolution scenes:

- tie up any remaining *major* plot threads.
- show the character, transformed and wiser, taking action in his new world.
- show a juxtaposition, or contrast, from the shadow self into the integrated self through new, stronger actions.
- may contain more reflection than action.
- are slower and calmer, lacking any urgency—unless you're writing a series in which you might end on a cliff-hanger note. In that case, you may choose to end with a climax scene rather than a final scene.

Though you must tie up the major plot points, you may leave one or more lingering questions in the minds of your readers. That's okay so long as they aren't the type of unanswered questions that keep your readers up at night feeling disappointed. Readers like closure, and unless you promise a sequel, it's better to deliver completion.

For memoir, the final scene may take a slightly different shape. There may be no plot points to tie up but merely a scene or two that shows the character living life after his climax, wiser and stronger for it.

In *The Glass Castle*, Jeannette Walls makes it to New York and begins her life in earnest. And surprisingly, she even stays in touch with her folks and siblings for the most part, though her mother ends up homeless off and on, and her father dies young. Jeannette shows us that she survived her childhood and became a functional member of society, holding jobs and getting married.

In *Night Film*, after all leads have revealed no criminal dirt on Cordova, McGrath puts together the final clues that he was unable to see during his pursuit. The clues point to a deeper, more psychological journey inside himself. With clear sight and a renewed sense of priorities to become a better father and journalist, he sees the clues that were always there and takes a journey to a remote Chilean village, where his final answer awaits him.

In *State of Wonder*, Marina returns home freed from the emotional strictures and fears that have kept her life small. She no longer thinks only of herself; she takes Anders straight to his family, and then, after witnessing a joyous reunion, she tells the driver to "go on." In that small moment it feels as though Marina is moving on, too, hopefully toward decisions and goals that will feed the happiness blooming within her.

In your final scenes, your character has overcome and transformed, leaving the reader with a feeling of having completed a meaningful journey.

IN SUMMARY

Action in end scenes bears the burden of getting your characters to the right place at the right time for one last confrontation. It facilitates the final play, in which your protagonist is powerful enough to triumph over the antagonist, leading to transformation. These scenes comprise the final quarter of your book.

When writing action in end scenes, keep in mind that:

- the character acts boldly and with determination when transitioning from intense middle scenes to ending scenes.
- the emotional stakes and intensity in every scene move ever higher as she prepares to confront her shadow one last time.
- the character engages in actions toward a specific goal that begin to reflect an integrated self.
- the character makes new plans for herself based on the integration of shadow.
- the character has a final confrontation with the shadow.
- the character takes new action in her "new world."
- tension is created through the dramatic question of whether the protagonist will succeed or fail.
- the antagonists have grown stronger and more determined, and have raised the stakes for the protagonist to an all-time high.

Part Two

EMOTION

CHAPTER EIGHT

EMOTION IN THE BEGINNING SCENES

Dwelling in the Shadow Realm

Scene types addressed: first scenes, contemplative scenes, dialogue scenes, romance scenes, suspense scenes

While action drives the engine of the story, emotion makes readers care about, and connect with, your characters. When the protagonist's inner workings are transparent, the reader's heart is filled with empathy, concern, and fear for him. Characters of all kinds, but especially protagonists, are ciphers for our experiences; that is to say, it's common for the reader to project herself into the lives of the people she reads about, to enter their minds and feel as though she is along for the ride.

Emotion is a catchall kind of word for the vast and varied feelings your characters will experience through the story's progression and how these feelings drive their story goals. As we mentioned in chapter two, the more complex your characters' feelings—and the less flat, clichéd, or stereotypical—the more real your characters and their experiences become to the reader. From past longings that haunt characters to newly kindled elation, fear, or love that unfolds in the story, emotions inform readers of the impact goals and events of the story have upon your character and his transformation. The term *emotion* also speaks to the feelings you will stir in your reader as she joins your characters on their journeys.

EMOTION IN THE BEGINNING

It's crucial to demonstrate characters' emotions in every scene—through their words, actions, and reactions; through minimal contemplation or thought; and even through the use of symbolic and visual imagery rather than shorthand "telling" language. In chapter two, we used the phrase "Demonstrate, don't lecture" as a reminder to avoid summarizing. This axiom is especially important when it comes to revealing emotion in characters. Don't simply tell the reader, "She was hurt." Instead, show what being hurt looks like. Does she fold into a ball in the corner of the room? Does that pain manifest in a physical way—as heat or a prickling in her body? Emotions exist in the realm of the body. The more you use sensory description and action to demonstrate emotion, the more the reader will feel what your character feels and thus become more deeply engaged.

Introducing Your Character's Strength, Longing, and Fear

In the beginning scenes of your story, you must introduce your character's emotional stance toward himself and his life, both his shadow side—his wounds, fears, and pain—and the desires that will draw him toward the light of change and growth. This means you will set up, through contemplation and dialogue, how your character feels about life as he knows it. Is his role in life a necessary burden? Is he chomping at the bit to break free? Is his life relatively simple and content? Does he have no real desire to change the status quo, though change is about to be foisted upon him? In the beginning, your protagonist's emotional state may be muddy or complex, full of conflicting emotions and uncertainty as well as hope, elation, or anticipation. What's most important is that you communicate how he feels or thinks about his life relatively quickly.

In Jacki Lyden's memoir *Daughter of the Queen of Sheba*, the author establishes two quick emotional details about her life in the beginning scenes: that her mother's mental health is fragile and that her stepfather is the word of law in their home, a fact she resents.

> Christ Jesus appeared to [my mother] as a white octopus, luminescent in the darkness, deep in the middle of the night in our small town of Menomenee, Wisconsin. … My stepfather was the one in charge, not God. He was a doctor in our provident town and owned a small hospital and clinic, which treated half the populace, who granted him authority over their lives. … Money walled us in, I thought. It afforded my stepfather a manner of universal disdain.

It's clear that Lyden feels confined by her stepfather's money because it gives him an air of entitlement that does not mesh with her own views on life. She also senses that his entitlement confines her mother, who, although mentally ill, Lyden considers to be interesting and bigger than life. In these beginning scenes, she determines her stepfather is the source of her unhappiness.

The beginning scenes, especially the first scene, equate to a first date, in essence, between protagonist and reader. You want your readers to wish for a second date—in other words, you want them to keep reading. Therefore, it's also important to depict your characters' strengths—their values and talents, even if they are only in raw, unpolished, potential form at this point—as quickly as possible, and to set up compelling circumstances and goals that draw readers in.

For example, in Hugh Howey's dystopian novel *Wool,* the first time readers meet Jules, the unwitting new pick for sheriff of the community, they are intrigued and engaged by this determined female mechanic. Jules dwells in the lower levels of the silo, a vertical, underground community constructed in a post-apocalyptic world. Before being elected sheriff, she serves as a mechanic, working to keep the silo's electrical and mechanical parts running. Jules is well respected by all who work with her; though she is not necessarily a warm and fuzzy person, she is strong-willed and kind. This is what the mayor and her deputy, Jahns, observe when they arrive to interview her.

> A young-looking woman in overalls, a hard hat on, brown braided hair hanging out the back, was leaning into a wrench nearly as long as she

was tall. Her presence gave the machines a terrifying sense of scale, but she didn't seem to fear them. She threw herself into her wrench, her body frightfully close to the roaring unit. ...

Our first impression of Jules is of a tough but feminine woman, a woman of complexity, perhaps.

Jules assumes the mayor and Jahns want a report on the problems with the power grid, so she begins to bring them up to speed in her matter-of-fact way that cuts through any bull. When Jules hears the mayor mutter under her breath that they came here to recruit her away from this, she retorts quickly: "And I thought I told you—or your secretary— not to bother. Not that I've got anything against what you do, but I'm needed down here."

Jules is a strong, dutiful person, but clearly the job of sheriff is no promotion to her; it carries pressure that she neither wants nor aspires to, and it takes her away from the work she's good at in the mechanical department, work that is necessary to the life and livelihood of the entire population of the silo. Moreover, she is only being asked to take this promotion because her friend Holston went out for "cleaning"— essentially a death by exile in the toxic air above ground, outside the silo. In just a few words and gestures, as well as a few well-rendered visual details, readers are introduced to a woman of strength, talent, and integrity; though she doesn't want this thankless job, she agrees to do it because the silo needs a sheriff, and she can't say no if it means helping those in need.

This doesn't mean Jules is a perfect person; she has secrets and flaws. But how she handles this difficult promotion—which draws her past her Point of No Return at the First Energetic Marker—will determine not only the course of her future, but also the fate of the silo.

The most appealing protagonists are those with a solid moral compass and a willingness to rise to a challenge, even when that situation brings unpleasant, scary, or unfamiliar feelings. In fact, the greatest novels, memoirs, and screenplays always elicit powerful emotions in both protagonist and reader. This doesn't mean you can't write a compelling novel about an antihero (Patrick Suskind's novel *Perfume*, about a serial killer driven by the perfect scent, comes to mind), but those books are a much tougher sell and require that the story and the other characters be extraordinarily compelling to make up for such a deficit.

Demonstrating the Protagonist's Longing

Most protagonists are driven by unconscious emotion in the beginning scenes—namely fear and longing—particularly once they are presented with the charged transition of the Point of No Return. Your protagonist may dream of a bigger life, wealth, fame, escape from unhappiness, or fulfillment of a long-held aspiration or relationship. She may wish to change circumstances or to fight forces that seek to direct her life for her. Whatever her longing is (and yes, there may be several), it will point you toward her short-term and long-term emotional goals. Your protagonist's longings should rise authentically from her experiences and history (otherwise known as backstory), which will inform what she wants and how she will choose to get it.

In *Wool,* Jules's longing in the beginning is for peace. She wants to stay in her happy life in the lower levels with the "family" she knows—the people she works with to keep the mechanics of the silo intact. By removing her from her known reality, deep in the dark belly of the silo, new longings are set into motion, shifting her goals. Once she passes through her Point of No Return, traveling toward the light of the upper levels of the silo and toward truths long hidden from her, a complex and interesting story unfurls that will test her mettle and push her to greater emotional highs and lows that force her to transform.

Identifying your protagonist's longing in the beginning is crucial in determining where she will be at the remaining Energetic Markers of the story. Though character goals can change throughout the story, if you know what the protagonist wants in the beginning, you know how to use the antagonist to throw obstacles against that goal.

Be careful to pick a longing large enough to drive your story. It should have weight and significance, and provide stakes for her to gain and lose along the way.

Longing in the Form of Romance or Sex

Even though your book does not fall within the romance genre, you may still have a romantic emotional storyline, unless your characters are something other than human. People need people, and the longing for connection, be it in the heart or in the loins, is part of the human condition and keeps readers engaged. In the beginning scenes, you may have a character longing for a partner he does not have, grieving the loss of one, or yearning to be reunited with one.

In books that are not in the romance genre, romance scenes, as defined in chapter three, serve the purpose of revealing more about your protagonist to the reader and also offering a short-term sense of emotional reward. Sex scenes in books that are neither romance nor erotica are also a useful way to provide temporary rewards in a story where the protagonist must tackle a great deal of adversity and obstacles. But romance and sex scenes should never be gratuitous—that is, characters shouldn't profess their love for one another unless it has been earned or unless another character proves to be a false love to your protagonist, setting him up for heartbreak later on. Sex for its own sake comes across as cheap or empty to the reader. In addition, many readers bring their personal judgments to bear on when and how often characters should engage in sexual activity. With all this in mind, use both the emotional and physical elements of the romance scene with care.

In the beginning scenes, you'll most likely show only a hint of a relationship longed for or a relationship in its fledgling stages. Or you might show a relationship already in decline or coming apart at the seams.

In a romance novel, the acquisition of the romantic partner will be the major goal for the protagonist, though there may be minor complications surrounding it as well.

Showing the Protagonist's Fears

Beneath longing, however, also lurks fear, especially in beginning scenes. Your character longs for several things, but she also carries the fear that these longings may not come to fruition (and may hold even more complicated subterranean feelings below that, such as fear of losing herself to a lover or fear of finding out the person isn't who she thought). Sometimes the character's longing may not be based in reality, and the dramatic action of the story will have to push her toward a more realistic goal or pull her head out of the clouds. Unless you're writing a story in which the character's fear is the focus—the character is the victim of kidnapping or is already in dire straits—this fear may be subtle. What you don't want to show is a character so terrified and timid that the reader is immediately annoyed or overly concerned. You want to show just a hint of fear: a flicker of anxiety as your protagonist watches her husband get on the airplane; a tremor of terror as an abusive character lashes out at your protagonist; a shiver of dread as she surveys a stormy sea. In most genres, fear should be subtle in the beginning scenes, because this is still an introduction, but hinting at a problem is a way of alerting the reader that something needs to change or that a big event may be on its way.

Sometimes what your character fears most in the beginning is change itself. Characters may not be leaping at adventure with arms wide open; that's certainly realistic, so it's okay if you have a character who would like nothing more than to stay the same (as Jules does in *Wool*). That doesn't mean you're going to let her stay safe, however.

Evoking Emotion in the First Scene

Now that you have a sense of the emotional state of a protagonist in the beginning scenes, let's refresh the criteria of a first scene.

- It introduces the character and demonstrates his dramatic action (his goal or longing).
- Both the setting and the character's feelings about it are introduced in an integrated way.

- It sets up conflict for what is to come by showing internal and external emotional turmoil in the character.
- Through dialogue and interactions, it reveals the character's emotional state.

Emotion at the Point of No Return

Every story will have a slightly different number of scenes and variation of scene types in the beginning, but your entire first act usually comprises about one-quarter of your total story. It's a brief stretch of time. You will have a first scene that introduces your protagonist's identity, the time and setting she is in, her emotional plot (what she wants), and the dramatic action that sets her emotional plot into being through an event or scenario. This event forces her through the First Energetic Marker, Point of No Return, at the quarter mark of your story, and it's a powerful doorway for your character. On the one hand, this doorway may entice with positive anticipation and possibilities of new scenarios that seem better than where your protagonist finds herself currently. On the other hand, it may also induce a quake of anxiety or even terror. She may even be forced or pushed through. Let's explore some of the scene types you may want to draw upon in your first scene and your Point of No Return.

Contemplative Scenes

Contemplation—characterized by thoughts, internal monologue, and slower actions—may seem like the ideal way to introduce the reader to your character in the beginning scenes; sometimes there is no better way to reveal a character than by telling a few basic facts. But be careful not to rely *only* on contemplative exposition, and definitely do not rely on large chunks of explanatory backstory. Instead, allow your character's backstory to seep out the cracks in his behavior, words, and actions.

Better yet, weaving small doses of your character's thoughts in and around dialogue or actions can create a contemplative scene with energy and tension.

For instance, in the novel *The Art Forger,* B.A. Shapiro reveals crucial backstory bits in her beginning scenes through just such an interweaving of contemplation, small actions, and dialogue. Protagonist Claire Roth is a painter, a fact the reader learns through concrete details in the story's opening. Claire is shown in her studio surveying her recently completed art and anticipating a visit from a well-known art dealer.

"I remove Tower, a highly realistic painting of reflections off the glass Hancock building … ." Claire's narrative voice tells us.

She walks around and identifies other details of her paintings of windows: "Large, small, old, broken, wood- and metal-framed." Though Claire stays contemplative, thinking about her unhappiness at having become known as "The Great Pretender" in the art world, her thoughts are interspersed with her movements around her studio, as she touches and observes her paintings. We get contemplation, but we don't get backstory or exposition overkill—just enough to whet readers' curiosity. Shapiro then teases out pieces of Claire's emotional backstory once the art dealer, Adrian Markel, appears on the scene. They begin to talk about a painting by a man named Isaac. Titled "Orange Nude," it has just sold.

This passage begins with Claire's internal narration.

> As everyone knows, I was the model for Orange Nude. Even though it's an abstraction, there's no denying my long, unmanageable red hair or the paleness of my skin and brown eyes. If I hadn't thrown it out the door when we broke up, I'd probably be living in a condo in Back Bay instead of renting in an industrial building in SOWA. But then again, I'm not the Back Bay type. "Don't tell me how much you got for it."
>
> "I'll spare you the pain. But the sale started me thinking about you, about the raw deal you got."

So now we know there is more to the story of Claire, the art world "pretender": She was romantically involved with Isaac, and they have since broken up. She also received some sort of "raw deal." Already, from the opening scene, the reader feels badly for Claire, and the emotional stakes of this visit increase. The reader roots for Markel to have something wonderful to offer Claire.

Claire is surprised by Markel's kind words. Markel continues to talk in the face of her stunned silence.

> "So I decided to come down and see what you've been up to," he continues. "Maybe I can help."

Shapiro doles out backstory information through an interweaving of contemplation, small character gestures, and dialogue to paint the emotional portrait of Claire, who is desperate but hopeful that she is about to be given a second chance. This yearning desperation forms the root of her emotional plot, and it becomes more complex when Markel does not, in fact, give her a show at his gallery but asks her to paint a reproduction of a Degas painting. Claire's excitement switches to disappointment, but her feelings are complicated; she needs the money he's offering, and she still holds out hope that any work for the famous Adrian Markel may lead to her dream of artistic success. This emotionally weighted call to change launches Claire through her Point of No Return. She's one step closer to being back in the art world but not yet close enough to her dream of artistic fulfillment.

In a single scene, Shapiro sets up a powerful emotional plot for Claire, who is torn between her past and her future, her desire for success and her fear that she may never get what she most wants. When she walks through that doorway, everything will change for her.

Novelists have the most leeway to create and shape a first scene and Point of No Return as they see fit—it's fiction, after all. However, if you are a memoir writer, your beginning scenes may start with more contemplation, thereby setting the tone for the narrative voice of your story and expressing unhappiness, a lack of awareness, or a yearning to live a different life or experience.

Using Dialogue to Reveal Emotion in the Beginning Scenes

Many writers fall into the habit of explaining and describing a lot in the beginning of a story, fearing that readers won't be able to follow along if they don't fill them in first. But dialogue is a wonderful way to reveal information in the beginning scenes without relying too much on summary, which can slow the pace at the wrong juncture. Every character is different in the beginning scenes, but most protagonists are tied to unresolved feelings, old hurts, and life choices they probably wish to change or undo. Occasionally a protagonist is perfectly happy at the beginning of a novel, but circumstances pull her out of this happiness and take her through a ringer of experience that provides her truer or more authentic happiness than what she thought she had. More often than not, however, your character will muddle through a state of uncertainty at the beginning of the story.

In a screenplay, the opening scenes depict the protagonist's state of instability and longing through how she speaks and acts, with very little room for expository narrative (or in screenplay terms, *voice-over*). In other words, dialogue scenes are perfect for screenplay (and fiction) beginnings. Such is the case for David O. Russell's screenplay *Silver Linings Playbook* (based on the novel by Matthew Quick). When we first meet the main character, Pat, he is in a bedroom at a mental hospital, speaking aloud in a rushed, apologetic way to a woman named Nikki—who is not there with him.

> "I lost all that. I blew it. But you also blew it. We can get it back. We're gonna get it back … ."

The choice of dialogue makes clear instantly that this is a man who has been through something emotionally difficult, something he feels responsible for, even though we don't yet know the circumstances. Moreover, he wants a second chance.

Pat tells the orderly and then the doctor calling for him to "wait" so he can finish his manic monologue, which helps the reader understand that he isn't mentally stable yet; nor has he recovered from whatever sent him to the mental hospital in the first place.

His mother shows up in the scene and argues with the doctors; she wants to take Pat out of the hospital against medical recommendation. "I don't want him to get used to the routine in here," she insists. "Eight months is long enough." We learn through dialogue that Pat has serious emotional issues, even mental illness. Worse, he's a grown man who moved back in with his parents after his marriage fell apart. Pat is clearly stuck in the past emotionally.

It's tempting to try to get all the possible information about your character's emotional state of mind across in the beginning scenes, especially the first scene, by using heavy exposition and historical explanations of the characters' backstory, but by doing so you'd be simply explaining or telling information to readers that the character herself has not yet demonstrated in action and words. Characters behave their way into explanation. Russell deftly offers the audience all the information needed to launch the emotional development of Pat, who is separated from his beloved Nikki but determined to right some wrong, who was institutionalized for eight months, and who has now been released against medical advice to live with his parents. We learn all of this in less than four screenplay pages (about the equivalent of two novel pages).

Whether you use dialogue or a weaving of dialogue, contemplation, and action to reveal your character's emotional state in the first scene and the Point of No Return is not as important as doing so without lingering on exposition or long backstory segues that explain too much.

Using Suspense and Conflicting Emotions to Evoke Emotion

Suspense scenes work differently depending on where you use them. In the beginning, you have to use suspense carefully. Since a hallmark of a suspense scene is that the antagonist is at least as strong as the protagonist, in beginning scenes we may have gotten only a peek at the antagonist, and therefore she (or the forces that act as antagonists) may not be in full power yet.

In beginning scenes, you can build a sense of anxiety into your character's emotional state, as well as set up the stakes of the Point of No Return—a point of powerful emotional intensity, choice, or change for your protagonist.

The more conflicting emotion your character has, the more suspense. In *The Art Forger*, what Aiden Markel asks Claire to do—paint a Degas reproduction—rests on the edge of illegality. And he'll pay her a huge sum of money to do it: $50,000. It's money Claire badly needs.

Markel takes on the role of antagonist in true Faustian style: With his smooth words, handsome looks, and confident promises, he urges Claire toward a threshold that conflicts with her own integrity.

Their dialogue becomes suspenseful once Claire realizes what he's asking.

> I don't break the stare. "I thought you said it was an opportunity to do good?"
>
> "The end is good. It's just the means that are a bit iffy."
>
> "Illegal?"
>
> "There's illegal and there's illegal."
>
> "And which one is this?"
>
> Markel looks across the room at the Degas and Pissarro.
>
> And now it all makes sense. "Oh" is all I can say.

At first, Claire's integrity is at the forefront, and the reader feels momentary relief: She's not going to do something illegal. She wouldn't stoop that low. But then Markel slings her the low ball: an offer to show twenty of her paintings nine months after she has finished this sketchy reproduction.

Claire's contemplation raises the emotional stakes and creates suspense.

The New York Times. Sales. Commissions. Studio visits from the Met. My heart actually hurts.

Claire's longing is palpable on the page, and though the chapter ends without her making a decision, the reader knows and even roots for her to take the offer; we want her to have what she deserves, and we are seduced by Markel's confidence that he can protect her should anything go awry.

In *Silver Linings Playbook,* once Pat gets into his mother's car with his equally disturbed friend Danny, the suspense of uncertainty is at play during the ride home. This scene shares some qualities with an escape scene because of the heightened sense of pressure and urgency created by Pat's mental state and his fast-talking friend. In the scene, Pat is emotionally changeable, bantering with Danny while his mother, Dolores, grows increasingly anxious about Danny's presence. When the hospital calls and tells her that Danny was not supposed to be released along with Pat, Pat manically tries to convince her it's okay and then grabs the steering wheel when she tries to turn back. It creates powerful, suspenseful anxiety that translates both on the page and in the resulting film.

Using Imagery to Create an Emotional Mood

Since beginning scenes don't allow you much room for explanation or history—because they need to rope the reader in quickly—you can use visual imagery and sensory description to set an emotional tone without having to state plainly what the characters are feeling.

A great example of this comes from Emily St. John Mandel's novel *Station Eleven,* which alternates among several settings and times: the collapse of civilization due to a worldwide pandemic flu, several time periods before the collapse, and fifteen years after it, when people have begun to rebuild and move on despite all that has been lost.

The novel opens by setting a somber, foreboding tone through the powerful use of imagery.

> The king stood in a pool of blue light, unmoored. This was act 4 of
> *King Lear*, a winter night at the Elgin Theatre in Toronto. Earlier in
> the evening, three little girls had played a clapping game onstage as
> the audience entered, childhood versions of Lear's daughters, and now
> they'd returned as hallucinations in the mad scene. The king stumbled
> and reached for them as they flittered here and there in the shadows.

Several details in this opening paragraph create an ominous, serious
feeling: the color of the "blue light" signifies sadness or depression, and
it's "unmoored"—as though it is a force of nature unleashed on the set,
or a poltergeist. Lovely little touches, such as the description of the king
as he "stumbled and reached" for the actresses playing Lear's daughters
"in the shadows," build a sense of foreboding.

And something terrible *does* happen, first in the scene, and later in
the larger plot.

> "Down from the waist they are Centaurs," he said, and not only was this
> the wrong line but the delivery was wheezy, his voice barely audible. He
> cradled his hand to his chest like a broken bird.

That image of the cradled hand like a "broken bird" is deeply portentous.
The actor who is playing Lear, Arthur Leander, is having a fatal heart attack, but the image also presages what is about to come that night: The
flu, which kills people within a day of contracting it, begins to spread
around the city.

These understated touches, which we explore further in Part Three,
help drop emotional hints without being heavy-handed or overbearing.

Ultimately your opening scenes must, in a very short period of
time, demonstrate your character's emotional state, her longings, and
her fears, in order to set her (and thus the reader) up to change over the
course of her journey.

IN SUMMARY

Beginning scenes bear the burden of introducing your character and what he considers his "normal" world, which includes how he feels about and interacts with the setting and time period. In the beginning scenes, in addition to dramatic action, you must also reveal his relationship to his goals, the antagonist, and other characters. When showing emotion in the beginning scenes, you want to:

- introduce the character's emotional relationship to his shadow and light.
- identify the character's fear, longing, and strength.
- demonstrate the character's motivation.
- reveal surface, and even hidden, emotional sides of the character.
- show how the character's feelings influence the action.
- show the character's emotion launched by the action
- show how the character's traits shape-shift into flaws, putting more pressure to bear against him.

CHAPTER NINE

EMOTION IN THE EMERGING MIDDLE SCENES

Testing the Self and Moving Toward the Light of Integration

Scene types addressed: suspense scenes, dialogue scenes, contemplative scenes, epiphany scenes

Emotion differs from action. Generally speaking, action causes an emotional effect in the character. The back-and-forth play between action and emotion creates a tighter bond with the reader than action alone. As the protagonist is faced with resistance and interference in the middle and finds herself unable to reach her goals, she reveals more and more of her inner truth.

For the first time, the protagonist begins to show cracks in her everyday mode of acting, speaking, and thinking. Action in middle scenes, detailed in Part One, not only serves to keep the reader interested and turning the pages but also reveals all the emotions of the character—even those that are hidden from her.

Scenes in the middle of a novel, memoir, or screenplay provide the testing ground and center of conflict where the protagonist is exposed from all sides. In the middle she is now confronted with more intense opposition, revealing her darker sides, weaknesses and flaws, false beliefs, and disingenuous actions. This resistance is not only for the entertainment of the reader; it also forces the protagonist to face those characteristics of herself that she is oblivious to or may prefer to keep hidden.

In the emerging middle, though the antagonism is intense, the challenges are lighter in comparison to the conflict that comes in the deeper middle. Before the character is able to successfully reach her goal, she must integrate all sides of herself, positive and negative, shadow and light. Before she can learn and change, first her hidden, adverse elements must be exposed. This painful opening up begins in earnest in the middle of the story. The deeper she journeys into the middle, the more the protagonist finds herself in the grip of her jealousy, resentment, bitterness, spitefulness, stubbornness, confusion, fear, and weakness—or whatever emotional flaw she embodies. The discovery of her unpleasant sides creates emotion, and emotion connects the reader to a story.

EMOTION IN THE EMERGING MIDDLE

In the new world of the emerging middle, the character's "normal" actions and perceptions no longer move him nearer to his goals or lead him to success. His feelings about and interactions with the new setting become opportunities to learn more about himself. Show emotion in middle scenes through his relationship with his dilemma, his goals, the antagonist(s), and other characters.

Transitioning from the Beginning to the Shadow Side of the Middle

In the beginning, the character seduces the reader by keeping the action exciting and holding back many of her darker aspects. By the middle, just as the reader commits to reading the entire story, the exotic new world demands that the character stretch, and by stretching she begins in earnest to reveal her flaws and weaknesses. For the reader to grasp who the character truly is, antagonists must provoke the protagonist into displaying all sides of herself.

In Part One, we discussed how dramatic action provides this provocation. In this chapter we explore the character's effect on the action, the effects the action has on the character, and also what each effect reflects about the character and how it contributes to her overall emotional transformation.

Emotional tension in a scene creates dramatic tension in the reader's mind: Will she or won't she succeed? That same tension creates emotion in the reader's heart: What effect will the character's success or failure have on her character growth?

Plot is how the events in a story directly impact the main character, and the effect her fears (shadow) and desires (light), which force her to act and react, have on the story events. Always, in the best-written stories, characters are emotionally affected by the events of the story and transformed by the dramatic action. This transformation makes a story meaningful. The dramatic action demands a goal; the character's emotional development demands growth.

Our earlier example, *The Night Circus*, begins the middle scenes with the grand opening of the circus, the venue where the life-or-death competition between the two major characters, Marco and Celia, takes place. Neither character knows the rules of the competition, and though Marco strives to uncover them in an early middle scene, he cannot find the answers. Finally, Celia's father, Hector Bowen (a.k.a. "Prospero the Enchanter"), who, because of an experiment gone wrong, is "no more than an apparition in the dimly lit tent," informs Celia of the rules in a dialogue scene.

> "The identity of your opponent does not matter."
>
> "It matters to me."
>
> Hector frowns, watching as she absently toys with the ring on her right hand.
>
> "It shouldn't," he says.

"But my opponent knows who I am, yes?"

"Indeed, unless your opponent happens to be profoundly stupid. And it is unlike Alexander to choose a profoundly stupid student. But it doesn't matter. It is better for you to do your own work without influence from your opponent, and without any of this collaborating as you call it."

He waves an arm at the Carousel and the ribbons shudder, as though the softest of breezes has wandered into the tent.

"How is it better?" Celia asks. "How is anything better than anything else here? How is one tent comparable to another? How can any of this possibly be judged?"

"That is not your concern."

"How can I excel at a game when you refuse to tell me the rules?"

The suspended creatures turn their heads in the direction of the ghost in their midst. Gryphons and foxes and wyverns stare at him with glossy black eyes.

"Stop that," Hector snaps at his daughter. The creatures return to their forward-facing gazes, but one of the wolves growls as it settles back into its frozen state. "You are not taking this as seriously as you should."

"It's a circus," Celia says. "It's difficult to take it seriously."

"The circus is only a venue."

"Then this is not a game or a challenge, it's an exhibition."

"It's more than that."

"How?" Celia demands, but her father only shakes his head.

"I have told you all the rules you need to know. You push the bounds of what your skills can do using this circus as a showplace. You prove yourself better and stronger. You do everything you can to outshine your opponent."

His explanation covers only the rules she needs to know in order for this part of the story to make sense. Holding back all the other details of the competition creates curiosity and a sense of mystery in the reader, and keeps the story moving forward without bogging down in minutiae. Hector's dialogue outlines for the reader both Celia's and Marco's long-term goal: to prove themselves "better and stronger" than their opponent.

By this point, early in the middle of *The Night Circus*, we understand all the basic elements of the plot:

- **WHO:** Celia and Marco
- **WHAT:** a competition in which each must show they are stronger than the other
- **WHERE:** the circus
- **WHEN:** now

The only missing piece is why. That unanswered question causes tension in the characters and keeps readers wondering what sort of disaster all this is leading to. We know disaster will be involved from the foreshadowing in the beginning—both Celia and Marco endure cold and cruel behavior from others early in their lives.

In a later scene in the emerging middle, Celia babysits the twins Poppet and Widget, who were born the night the circus opened. Celia learns that the now-four-year-old twins have special abilities to see details that others cannot: Poppet sees things in the stars, and Widget sees things about people. When Celia learns of Widget's supernatural ability, she asks if he can see anything about her.

> Widget squints at her while he chews his popcorn.
>
> "Rooms that smell like powder and old clothes," he says. "A lady that cries all the time. A ghost man with a frilly shirt that follows you around and—"
>
> Widget stops suddenly, frowning.
>
> "You made it go away," he says. "There's nothing there anymore. How did you do that?"
>
> "Some things are not for you to see," Celia says.

Though not yet obvious, this scene shows Celia gaining an understanding about herself in a new, clearer way. When Widget realizes that his abilities have been blocked by someone or something, at first we wonder if Prospero hindered his vision. As Celia speaks the final line of dialogue to Widget, she addresses the reader at the same time. Some things are not for us to see, either. This short section of dialogue provides us with the only information about Celia's mother and Celia's backstory from her point of view in the entire story. The line "A lady that cries all the time" provides an understanding of what Celia's life was like before coming to live with her father.

The dialogue between Celia and Widget is an emotional moment because we long for this fascinating and emotionally closed-off young woman to take us deeper into her heart. By preventing us access, we better understand her emotional development arc. Yes, she must win the competition—the action plot. She also must open her heart if she's ever going to satisfy her need for love—the emotional plot.

The opening part of the middle is the perfect place to slow down the action and reveal more of the inner landscape of the character and details of the new world. The reader, having reached the middle, is now committed to read to the end and willing to read slower scenes to better know the characters and this new world.

The dialogue in this scene switches to description about the fire in the courtyard that was lit at the opening ceremonies and has burned steadily ever since, gleaming "along the edges of the tents, casting dancing shadows of patrons across the striped fabric." At this point, Celia ties the seemingly disparate events of opening night together in her mind for both herself and for the reader: how the lighting of the bonfire set in motion something "that impacted the entire circus and everyone within it ... including the newborn twins." In that moment, Celia senses the magnitude of what's coming and what will be demanded of her. She resolves to keep the twins near, and the scene ends with a secret and the promise of the magic yet to come.

Showing how a character transforms over the course of the entire story is integral to the emotional plot. Showing each step in that internal progression is an essential element in every scene. The protagonist's emotional transformation takes place over time and culminates at the end of the story in a lasting change. It can be plotted from the beginning to the end of the story scene by scene.

Incorporate the emotion plot into every scene by:

- revealing another aspect of her personality and belief system.
- adding another layer of complexity to the traits and flaws assigned to her in the beginning.
- describing sounds, scents, and sights that are specifically meaningful and insightful to the character who is hearing, smelling, and seeing.
- characterizing the protagonist's actions and choosing words in dialogue and how she says them to relate specifically to her heart and mind.
- showing how she interacts with the world and other characters around her and how she's feeling in relationship to the interactions though her body language, responses, and internal sensations.

Integrating Emotion into Scenes Through the Character's Longing and Fear

How do the following two lists differ, and how are they the same?

honest	angry
courageous	frustrated
deceitful	pensive
stingy	apologetic
frugal	defensive
shy	happy

Each list originates in the character. The first is a list of character traits. The latter is a list of character emotions.

Character traits are all the aspects of the character's behavior and attitudes that make up his personality. Character traits are usually reflective of his upbringing. Character traits are made up of strengths and weaknesses, also known as flaws. Character *flaws* are limitations, deficiencies, or weaknesses in the character that interfere with his ability to achieve his goals.

Emotions represent the character's reaction to what's happening around and to him.

Character emotional transformation is the process of overcoming or changing a negative or shadow trait that holds back the character from what he wants in life and prevents him from being whole. Emotional transformation and emotion are different though closely related, and each one represents a unique, essential scene element: Incorporating the character's emotions of longing and fear in scene supports the overall development of his emotional transformation as he moves toward the integration of light and shadow and full emotional maturity.

In *The Night Circus*, both Celia and Marco are emotionally closed off. The way each of them spends their early lives in the beginning of the story is gruesome and lonely. The introduction of the twins in the first part of the middle brings light to an otherwise bleak and shadowy story. They introduce emotion to an otherwise barren emotional landscape.

The way in which both Celia and Marco are forced to grow and transform in order to seize their happy ending represents their emotional transformation plot, which travels from the beginning of the story all the way to the end.

At the scene level, emotion is evoked through challenging dramatic action that forces the protagonist to display a range of emotional reactions. Readers identify with a character through emotion, and when rendered well it actually pulls readers all the way into the story so that they become the character.

Emotions displayed by the character as he reacts to the action fluctuate within each scene and are usually transitory and fleeting. Showing your character's emotions shift and change is an essential element in every scene. Depict characters expressing and displaying honest and recognizable emotions. The most powerful way to connect with readers is by allowing them to experience the emotion for themselves. How a character reacts often is reflective of the burden he carries from his backstory.

The award-winning screenplay *Winter's Bone* thrusts seventeen-year-old Ree in the middle of violence, which is foreshadowed in the beginning of the story when Ree slaughters a deer, when Ree's best friend's new husband threatens physical punishment, and when Uncle Teardrop warns Ree not to ask the wrong people about her father's whereabouts or she could end up "et by hogs, or wishing you was."

Anticipation of the evil about to befall Ree in her search for her father—the action plot—creates great tension in the audience. They worry about the emotional damage, not to mention physical harm and possible death, this young girl must suffer crossing into the emerging middle and exotic world of the unknown. That she's taking these risks in an attempt to provide for her young siblings and vacant mother emotionally connects Ree to the audience. At this point, early in the middle of the story, the audience moves nearer to the edge of their seats.

Conflict, Tension, and Suspense

Conflict is established when an antagonist interferes with the protagonist's forward movement. The suspense comes from not knowing what's going to happen next or whether the protagonist or the antagonist will win. Tension is a felt response from the heart about what effect the conflict and the protagonist's success or failure will have both on her emotional transformation at the overall plot level and her emotions at the scene level.

Active conflict is created when a character wants something and an antagonistic force stands in her way of getting it. Active conflict points more to the action plot that originates outside the character: She moves toward her goal, and something blocks her forward progress.

Tension, on the other hand, points more to the emotional plot because tension originates inside the character. The further she stretches as she strives for something, the tighter she becomes and the more emotional stress she feels when rebuked. This emotional stress creates tension in the character and, when the truth of that tension is effectively conveyed, readers experience the tension, too.

In *Winter's Bone,* we know something bad is about to happen, but the suspense comes in not knowing just how bad it will be. Suspense causes tension in readers, which emotionally engages them and keeps them alert.

The emerging middle begins when Ree enters the yard of the family her uncle warned her against. Ree feeds a donkey an apple that has rolled out of its reach. The sweetness of her action is starkly contrasted by the appearance of Little Arthur, a major antagonist who demands an explanation as to why Ree is there. The threat of harm, and the risk of never finding her father, creates suspense and emotional tension that is felt in every action taken and word spoken.

Tension builds in the scene as we understand Ree must undergo another, more treacherous crossing. If she's ever going to find her father, she must confront Thump, a man who "scares [her] way more than the rest." The crackle of each dry leaf and dead tree branch underfoot as she makes her way to her doom sends chills of suspense, anxiety, and tension down our spines. That she moves ever forward toward what she hopes will help her find her father demonstrates her courage and persistence and her strong belief that family helps out each other in times of need.

The Character Begins to See Her Shadow

The character's emotional transformation forges a connection between the reader and the story. This transformation comprises more than simply how a character develops and transforms physically and intellectually, outfoxing and out-thinking and outperforming an antagonist. Readers must also feel a connection through the development of a character's emotional maturity. In other words, how a character finds and ultimately uses emotional balance to his advantage provides connection, identification, and interest.

First, however, he learns the hard way that he does, in fact, need to grow and change. That need to change is usually incited by character trait(s) established earlier in the story. Those traits may have served him well in his ordinary world, but now, in the exotic world of the middle, they begin to reveal their shadow side and flip from strengths into flaws.

Transformation doesn't happen automatically, and deep change isn't an inevitable gift bestowed for having suffered and survived a crisis. Transformation requires a resounding and full-hearted commitment by the protagonist to change, because before he can transform, he first must become conscious of his strengths and weaknesses. Each obstacle and antagonist in the action plot provides the protagonist with opportunities to learn about himself and thus advance his emotional plot.

Here's a sample of character traits turned into flaws:

TRAITS	FLAWS
Competent and in charge	Control freak
Sensitive and caring	Always the victim; unable to take responsibility for actions
Firm and to the point	Argumentative and short tempered
Inventive	A liar and a cheat
Dependable and consistent	Stubborn
Decisive	Always has to be right
Thorough	Perfectionist
Careful	Procrastinator
Tells it like it is	Sits in judgment

The main character's flaw establishes his level of emotional maturity and points to the potential for growth or transformation. His flaw also creates tension and conflict by interfering with his ability to achieve his goal, and by riling up his emotions.

Because the antagonists in the middle define the rules of the exotic world, the protagonist is no longer in familiar territory. What would have served Ree well in her "normal" world no longer works here in the mysterious world of the antagonists; in fact, the traits she possessed at the beginning could get her killed now.

Well aware of Ree's determination, the viewer immediately fears she is not going to heed her uncle's ominous warning to stay home, nor will she give up no matter how evil her antagonists. In other words, Ree's emotional makeup creates tension and anticipation, and the audience wonders how the character flaw demonstrated or implied at the beginning of the story will interfere and cause her to stumble more and more often in the middle. Ree's positive trait of determination switches to the flaw of bullheadedness, especially now that she's angry.

> **MERAB:** Thump knows you were in the valley, child. With Megan. And at Little Arthur's. He knows what you want to ask, and he don't want to hear it.
>
> **REE:** And that's it? He ain't gonna say nothing to me?
>
> **MERAB:** If you're listening, child, you got your answer.
>
> *Merab turns her back and walks toward her house. Ree calls after her.*
>
> **REE:** So, I guess come the nut-cutting, blood don't really mean shit to the big man. Am I understanding that right?
>
> *Merab spins on her heel and gets up into Ree's face.*
>
> **MERAB:** Don't you dare. Don't I want you to listen to me, child. You need to turn around and get yourself home.
>
> *Merab turns and walks back to her house. As she reaches the doorstep, she turns back towards Ree.*
>
> **MERAB:** Don't you make me come out here and tell you again!
>
> *Merab enters the house and slams the door. As Ree stomps away, Merab eyes her suspiciously from the window.*

We are now bubbling with anticipation to learn just how stubborn Ree is. However, back home, before she is given a chance to come up with an action plan of her own, she is forced to react as her neighbor, who is also Thump's relative, hauls her to his truck. The emotion elicited in her frantic attempts to hold tight to the porch railing and prevent him from removing her from her home heightens as she screams for her little brother to go inside. Her response to the action taken against her gives both her and the audience a deeper understanding of the pain her stubborn shadow side has caused and, more important, the pain she could ultimately bring to those she loves the most—her family.

Ree's neighbor takes her to a burned-out house, where he confirms that her "Dad's up there burnt to a crisp." We fear that every step forward she takes will be her last, until both Ree and the audience, at the same moment, come to understand that she has been deceived; she learns that "it must have been a year since that place blew," and that her father could not have died there. We are riveted to the story through the suspense of not knowing if she's going to persist or switch strategies to save the family farm, now that she believes her father to still be alive. Either way, we fear for her.

The Character Reveals Other Sides of Herself as She Engages with Allies and Secondary Characters

The beginning of *Winter's Bone* clearly and quickly establishes why the story and the character's successful completion of her goal should matter. At first, we see only the light sides of Ree: her commitment to her family, her kindness to animals, her take-charge attitude, her stubborn persistence in caring for her mother and siblings.

Ree's younger siblings and mother represent her motivation to take action without thought to the consequences. Her fear of losing them keeps her going even in the territory of the middle, when conflicts multiply and tension grows.

The emotions she kept in check in the beginning of the story start to unravel in the chaos and uncertainty of the unfamiliar world of the middle. The extent to which you reveal the character's emotions sends the reader deeper into her point of view.

In *A Tale of Two Cities*, Sydney Carton is the protagonist because he is the only character who is truly transformed by the action of the story. This novel contains many plots—political, historical, action, emotion, theme, romance, mystery, and suspense—and Sydney's emotional plot is nearly hidden in all the twists and turns of the other competing plots. Though he is the protagonist, he is not introduced until three-quarters into the beginning of the novel. At that point we are given only this description, in which he is not even named: "the wigged gentleman who had all this time been looking at the ceiling of the court." However, in the middle scenes in which Sydney appears, we gain a much deeper understanding of who this observant and compassionate man truly is, often with the aid of secondary characters.

At the beginning of the middle, we are immediately thrust into scene, observing Sydney drinking copious amounts of alcohol with a damp towel draped over his steaming head as he "extract[s] the essence from a heap of statements." He is preparing a legal case for the Attorney General, Sydney's longtime employer, who will then take credit for Sydney's work.

In the beginning, readers see only Sydney's keen observational abilities and propensity for slovenly and drunken behavior, but in the middle his character traits are expanded. We learn his strength is his intelligence, and we overhear his disastrous self-talk and how much he hates himself. We conclude that he may be self-medicating his manic-depression with whiskey.

Through dialogue between Sydney and the Attorney General, we learn how Sydney views himself. This scene, written from the viewpoint of the Attorney General, reveals yet another dimension to the protagonist while also discussing the key character traits in Sydney's ultimate transformation.

Introducing a longtime relationship—in this case, the one between Sydney and the Attorney General—allows Dickens to reveal sides of the protagonist's backstory as they converse over work. The Attorney General notes: "'The old seesaw Sydney. Up one minute and down the next; now in spirits and now in despondency!'" He follows this by saying, "'[Y]our way is, and always was, a lame way. You summon no energy and purpose.'"

We quickly catch on that the Attorney General is using Sydney and manipulating him rather than inspiring him to do better or to think better of himself; he is dragging Sydney down. And when he wonders, "How do I do what I do?" we cheer as Sydney replies, "Partly through paying me to help you, I suppose." But just as quickly, Sydney criticizes himself while uplifting the speaker: "You were always in the front rank, and I was always behind."

This one dialogue scene and interaction with a minor secondary character exposes the full extent of Sydney's limitation and establishes brilliantly the conflict between Sydney's potential and his downfall, showing the reader just how destitute and wounded and self-deprecating he is. For all intents and purposes, he is his own worst enemy.

In that last line of dialogue we are given a glimpse into what ails Sydney.

A character flaw—in Sydney's case, his belief that he was "always behind" and not "front rank"—is a coping mechanism that arises from the loss of the character's original state of perfection. This loss often occurs in the character's backstory. The middle is the place to show how deeply this flaw runs and how painful it will be for the character to face her shadow side.

The character stores the emotion created by the loss that occurred in her backstory. Her flaw is designed to compensate for a perceived vulnerability or a sense of insecurity. No matter how confident, every major character demonstrates lessons learned from the wound that was inflicted in her backstory and is now lodged in her core belief system. In reaction, she often surrenders some or all of the authority over her own life to someone or something else.

Emotion at the Rededication

The character's understanding of where he's been and where he's headed halfway through the story, as well as the subsequent push forward toward his goal(s), constitutes the most powerful recommitment scene in the entire story: the Rededication.

The scene or scenes at the Rededication Marker establish where the character is when he reaches the halfway point of the story in relationship to both the action plot and the emotional plot. This turning point helps reconnect the reader to the story by making clear what is important now. Writers often falter at this juncture because several (or many) subplots have formed for secondary, often antagonistic, characters. All of these subplots need to be considered, deepened, and intensified. To keep writing toward your goal of finishing your story when the primary plot gets tangled in subplots, plot twists, and characters all clamoring for a spotlight requires a commitment that transcends logic and demonstrates a belief in the possibilities. The main character also experiences the challenges of moving forward when success seems impossible and highly improbable at the midpoint.

This section of a story often proves difficult for readers, too. Thus the reader benefits from the clarity of the Second Energetic Marker, which will help him determine the levels of importance for the characters and the action. Every moment in a story is an opportunity to commit to moving forward, and the Second Energetic Marker is a great time to redefine what is important to the character now and why she continues to put one foot after another, deeper and deeper into the great unknown. As the reader receives hints of the perils awaiting the protagonist, he needs to know (and, moreover, to believe) the character's motivation for going forward into sure danger and possible death.

In *A Tale of Two Cities*, the Second Energetic Marker plays out in one dialogue scene where our protagonist professes his undying commitment to Miss Lucie Manette, a woman he admires and loves but knows he can never have because of his lowly behavior.

Through dialogue, he explains she is "'the last dream of my soul. In my degradation, I have not been so degraded but that the sight of you ... has stirred old shadows that I thought had died out of me.'"

He goes on to explain how she inspires him to "'strive afresh,'" "'begin anew,'" and "'shake off sloth and sensuality,'" and that he wishes for her to "'know that you inspired it [and] have reclaimed me.'" With the poignancy and honesty in his declaration of love, he continues: "'Let me carry through the rest of my misdirected life, the remembrance that I opened my heart to you, last of all the world.'"

She promises to keep this last confidence of his life "'... reposed in [her] pure and innocent breast, and that it [will lie] there alone, and will be shared by no one. ...'"

Sydney and Lucie become bonded. His last words in the scene are a dramatic foreshadowing of what is to come at the end: "[T]hink now and then that there is a man who would give his life, to keep a life you love beside you!"

In Sydney's interactions with Lucie, we come to appreciate a much different side of him than was revealed through his longtime acquaintance. When he dedicates himself to her by professing, "For you and for any dear to you, I would do anything," he is verbalizing what he'd already committed to himself and to the reader—his heart.

As shown in the scene examples throughout this chapter, conflict is a formidable force even in the emerging middle. Each trial and test the protagonist undergoes drags him nearer to the darkest part of the middle.

In *The Night Circus*, several seemingly episodic transition scenes lead up to the Second Energetic Marker. These scenes serve to move the reader from the emerging middle into the deeper middle, and help shift between subplots and the primary plot.

One transition scene depicts a short funeral, symbolizing the death of the old to make way for the new. The scene contains more narrative summary than active scene elements, which makes the quiet revelation between two secondary characters about problems in the circus even more chilling.

> "It will come apart," Tsukiko says after a long while. Isobel does not need to ask what she means. "The cracks are beginning to show. Sooner or later it is bound to break."

The ominous warning in this transition scene—"It will come apart"— also serves as a promise to the reader: Tension, disaster, and big problems are coming. Having a clearer idea of the stakes in the story at the midpoint causes the reader to wonder if and how both contestants will continue when they, too, understand the risks involved in going forward.

Another recommitment scene follows. The twins, Poppet and Widget, meet Bailey, a thoughtful boy who attends the circus as a spectator. Confused about the fortune teller's vision of his future, Bailey begins the dialogue scene "off for a walk" with the twins. They exchange names and get to know each other, discussing "the big cats" and other details about the circus. Bailey learns of Poppet's "strange" and magical ability of seeing things before they happen. After experiencing an "impossible" circus ride at the end of this scene, Bailey is forever changed.

> ... it feels as though the Bailey who entered the circus was an entirely different person than the one leaving it now. ... [H]e is sure that the Bailey he is now is closer to the Bailey he is supposed to be than the Bailey he had been the day before. ... In his dreams, he is a knight on horseback, carrying a silver sword, and it does not really seem that strange after all.

The last line in this excerpt foreshadows what is to come at the end of the story. Of course, the reader doesn't know this yet. What he does know is that things are changing. The old ways are dying, and new dreams are emerging.

So, what of the fate of our two young magicians, Celia and Marco, the opponents in the contest at the center of the novel?

Finally, at the true Second Energetic Marker, in what could be considered a lay-of-the-land scene, the two main characters meet each other for the first time. This scene orients the reader to their world as they grapple with the emotional conflicts of coming to know each other both as competitors and much more.

Both Celia and Marco reveal, if not to each other then at least to the reader, what is most important to them. They openly and honestly face, discuss, and demonstrate their relative strengths and weaknesses as masters of manipulation and enchantment. Early in the scene, Celia still has one foot in the old world of not knowing who she is competing against and the other foot firmly in the new world of discovering his identity. She is "still not certain what to make of [her opponent]."

Celia also makes clear what she is and is not willing to do for others. She tells Marco:

> "When I was old enough to understand [my mother taking her own life], I promised myself I would not suffer so for anyone. It will take a great deal more than that charming smile of yours to seduce me."
>
> But when she looks back, the charming smile has disappeared.
>
> "I'm sorry you lost your mother in such a way," Marco says.

We then witness Marco's emotional reaction to her declaration, and we learn more about the competition and what each of them knows about the part the other plays.

> "I think it strange we were prepared in drastically different ways for the same challenge," Marco says. He looks at Celia's hand again, though

now there is clearly nothing amiss, no indication that it was stabbed only moments ago.

"I suspect that is part of the point," she says. "Two schools of thought pitted against each other, working within the same environment."

"I confess," Marco says, "I don't fully understand the point, even after all this time."

"Nor do I," Celia admits. "I suspect calling it a challenge or a game is not entirely accurate. I've come to think of it more as a dual exhibition."

Marco follows this dialogue with an internal delight: "Knowing that she thinks of the circus as an exhibition comes as a pleasant surprise, as he had stopped considering it antagonistic years ago."

Thanks both to the warning in the earlier transition scene between Tsukiko and Isobel, and to the violence Celia and Marco have suffered, we know that they don't have a full grasp of what is going on with the circus, and we worry for them, especially as the scene progresses and we witness their reactions when he takes her hand to help her up.

> It is the first time he has touched her bare skin. The reaction in the air is immediate. A sudden charge ripples through the room, crisp and bright. The chandelier begins to shake.

The two of them are equally shaken by the other's touch, and in their final exchange in the scene we understand that they have both rededicated themselves to the challenge and, though pitted together in a life-and-death struggle, their hearts have committed to each other.

"Misdirection is one of my strengths," Marco says.

"It won't be as easy now that you have my attention."

"I like having your attention," he says. "Thank you for this. For staying."

Each of these minor and major recommitment scenes at the Second Energetic Marker create consequences that will need to be addressed by further action. None of them are big, external, dramatic action scenes. They also are not contemplative scenes, because the characters interact with each other, make commitments through dialogue, and provide a clear understanding about where they are both emotionally and physically as they move into the deeper middle of the story.

In each of the scenes analyzed, characters open up beyond a simple exchange of verbal information to include insight into what's really affecting them about the interaction. When they open up in this way, it points to the thematic significance of the story, deepens the reader's understanding of the characters with real-time action (though not particularly rapid paced), reveals plot information, provides "digestible bites" of backstory, and includes emotional significance of the interactions to the characters. Thus each of these scenes could be considered both dialogue scenes and recommitment scenes.

These recommitment scenes are each driven from the heart, binding the characters and the reader more tightly. At the Second Energetic Marker in *The Night Circus*, all of the aforementioned characters either subtly or obviously recommit and rededicate themselves to continue, in spite of the subtle or not so subtle warnings that their lives are about to get much more complicated and dangerous.

When your protagonist rededicates herself to her goal at the halfway point, she feels the energy in her life rise in significance. This energetic surge is a warning to the protagonist and reader both to wake up and prepare for something big.

IN SUMMARY

The middle scenes are the testing ground and center of conflict designed to reveal all the emotions of the character, even those that are hidden. This is the time when the character's traits in the beginning often switch to flaws as more pressure is put to bear against her.

Emotion in the middle scenes:

- shows how the character influences the action.
- shows how the action launches the character's emotion.

- uses epiphany scenes to force the character into new understandings of herself.
- uses suspense scenes to create excitement and connect emotionally with readers.
- uses dialogue scenes to reveal nuances about the characters by what they say and don't say, and by what others say about them.
- shifts the character from the person she shows herself to be in the beginning scenes to the shadow side she reveals in the middle scenes.
- shows the character's longing and fear that sends her toward the light (though the shadow comes with her).
- reveals character as she begins to see her shadow and deal with its consequences.
- demonstrates character as she reveals other sides of herself and engages with allies and secondary characters.
- uses a recommitment scene to help establish where the character is at the halfway point of the story in relationship to the action.

CHAPTER TEN

EMOTION IN THE DEEPER MIDDLE SCENES

Stretching the Self and Moving Toward the Darkness of Disintegration

Scene types addressed: transition scenes, recommitment scenes, dialogue scenes, lay-of-the-land scenes, crisis scenes, epiphany scenes

A major turning point separates emerging middle scenes, where the protagonist is tested, from deeper middle scenes, where she is stretched, often until she snaps. Always, the Rededication Marker signifies the end of the emerging middle and the beginning of the deeper middle. The protagonist looks past fears and doubts and recommits to her goal(s), despite the uncertain outcome. There are other lesser moments in a story when the character recommits to a course of action; however, the scene at the halfway mark earns the status of an actual Energetic Marker because her rededication points in a straight line to the next major Energetic Marker, the Dark Night, which presents both a crisis and a disastrous setback.

Once the story moves into the deeper middle, the protagonist is confronted by evermore powerful antagonists and pummeled by forces intent on preventing her success. The energy of the story rises as she is forced to stretch in response to the conflict, tension, suspense, excitement, and/or curiosity growing in every scene. As she stretches, she identifies her strengths and weaknesses and pinpoints both her harmful and helpful behaviors.

The consequences of poor decisions, misguided direction, stubborn willfulness, and wrong thinking lead to action, both through time passing and through plot movement. Scenes in the deeper middle become more energized by the often severe and punishing challenges the protagonist encounters. Outer and inner forces test, dare, and hinder the main character from getting what she wants. This push and pull creates friction. The more intense the friction, the hotter the fire burns. The rising tension has an affect on the character, which begins to change her over time. Because of this, writers are often viewed as alchemists because they seemingly possess the miraculous power to change the form, appearance, or nature of their main character(s). Opposing action that transmutes the character in depth over time magically produces meaning—the alchemist's gold.

In the beginning, the kindling is laid, and in the emerging middle, the fire is lit. Now, in the deeper middle, the fire roars through activities, movement, dialogue, and external successes and failures. The flames are so intense that they burn off the dross of the character and reveal her inner gold. The final transformation, as the protagonist emerges a changed individual, is reserved for the final quarter of the story at the Triumph. But in the deeper middle, your job is to keep the heat on high.

EMOTION IN THE DEEPER MIDDLE

In Part One, we discussed the intensifying darkness of the deeper middle, which comes externally from antagonists, villains, and tricksters, and from all the dark forces in society that are intent, either consciously or unconsciously, on preventing the protagonist from reaching her goal.

In this chapter, we want to show the affect the antagonist(s) (both internal and external) have on the protagonist as she is relentlessly challenged.

The Character Gets a Taste of Her Integrated Self

The darkness that comes internally from the protagonist's personal shadow is often revealed as a fatal flaw. For the protagonist to reach her goal and triumph at the end, she must face her foes, but she must also face herself. The unique plot of your story determines what she needs to learn in the middle of the story and the degree to which she must change to achieve her goals. In all stories, character transformation is cumulative and spans the entire narrative. The learning-growth-change-transformation cycle plays out in distinct ways as shown in the beginning, the emerging middle, the deeper middle, and the end.

In the beginning, each character demonstrates a level of emotional maturity through the introduction of vital character traits: light traits that support her success and happiness, and dark traits that prevent her from achieving what she wants in life.

In the emerging middle and deeper middle of the story, as the protagonist takes action in pursuit of her goals and meets with interference, she reveals more deeply how these traits work for and against her. External antagonists push her deeper into adversity and conflict, which thrusts her deeper into herself until she arrives at a point of complete despair and sacrifices everything at the Dark Night.

- **BEGINNING:** Introduce character traits.
- **EMERGING MIDDLE AND DEEPER MIDDLE:** Deepen and break traits.
- **END:** Reveal a changed and transformed character.

The conflict between what the character wants and what stands in her way internally and externally allows the reader to see all of the character's different sides. The tension created in the character and in the reader at each point of conflict creates excitement as readers hope she succeeds and fear she will fail based on her previous setbacks and wrong turns. Uncertainty about the outcome connects the reader strongly to the story.

In a twister scene at the beginning of *Winter's Bone*, Ree demonstrates her disrespect for authority through her dialogue and behavior, and shows herself to be defensively independent even after Sheriff Baskin delivers his stunning news.

> **SHERIFF BASKIN:** You know your daddy's out on bond, don't you?
> **REE:** So what?
> **SHERIFF BASKIN:** Looks like he's been cooking again.
> **REE:** I know that's the charges you laid on him, but you ain't proved it on him. You got to prove it every time.
> **SHERIFF BASKIN:** Well, that won't be no hard thing to do. But that ain't even why I'm here. His court date's next week, and I can't seem to turn him up.
> **REE:** Maybe he sees you and ducks.
> **SHERIFF BASKIN:** That could be. But where you all come into this is, he put this house here, and your timber acres up for his bond.
> **REE:** He what now?
> **SHERIFF BASKIN:** Jessup signed over everything. If he doesn't show at trial, see, the way the deal works is, you all gonna lose this place. You got some place to go?
>
> *Shock courses through Ree, but she tries to mask it.*
>
> **REE:** I'll find him.
> **SHERIFF BASKIN:** Girl, I've been lookin'.
> **REE:** I said I'll find him.

Having earlier signed up for an ROTC event at school, Ree intends to join the military, but as we can see here, her belligerent emotions call into question her ultimate readiness for a life that demands compliance and respect.

In the emerging middle, Ree defies authority and every warning as scene by scene she independently crosses over into one forbidden territory after another. By walking onto Little Arthur's property and into his house and then all the way to Thump's yard, she deepens the reader's understanding that her initial character traits are not simply random but are hardwired for survival.

In a suspense scene in the deeper middle, Ree searches for Thump at the cattle stockyard. When she disrespects him by shouting out in public, we understand that nothing will stop her from finding her father. When she follows up by returning to his house, she knows, and we know, too, that this time she's gone too far.

The Character's Longing (or Goal) Appears to Be Within Reach

The scenes in the deeper middle before the Dark Night Energetic Marker represent the darkest and most perilous time for the protagonist in the entire story so far. The protagonist loses as often or more than she wins and is often pushed backward. Even so, she gains confidence each time she confronts yet another challenge and finds a way around or through, managing always to move yet another step forward.

The tension in the scenes between the two middle markers builds, scene by scene, as challenges take on more meaning and the negative consequences turn more dire, even as hope for a positive outcome burns ever brighter in the heart of the protagonist and the reader alike.

The Dark Night is a point of release that forces the protagonist to view her goal(s) and her life differently. The clarity she gains through the burning away of all her illusions gives her the ability to face the greatest challenge at the end of the story and not only to survive but to triumph.

In scenes in the deeper middle, refrain from overusing descriptions, details, backstory, and explanations that may slow down the pace of the story. Only include what is absolutely necessary about the character, her emotion, and her goal to inform that particular scene. Traveling lightly with streamlined and focused scenes moves the story forward more quickly and with more urgency. Also, by withholding details, the reader is drawn deeper into the story in the hope of relieving the suspense of not knowing what is going to happen next.

The better you are at creating tension through the use of antagonists in the middle of your story, the more paramount your grasp of the true measure of your character's motivation. In order for readers to believe the protagonist would keep moving forward even in the face of all of this adversity, you must create motivation strong enough to sustain her during the darkest times.

Often writers find that the motivation they set up for their character at the beginning of the story isn't strong enough to justify the character's commitment through the middle of such a challenging journey. Perhaps what you first envisioned is enough to get her moving, to cause her to act, to initiate change, and to guide her forward. As you dig for a more substantial, more universal, and more emotionally connective motivation, the source of the original motivation is a potential place to dig.

Determine whether you started your story with an internal motivation or an external one. Does she have to win to prove to herself she's a winner (internal)? Or does she have to win to put food on the table for her family (external)? Once you know whether her motivation originates from within her or outside of her, look at the other side of the motivation in the deeper middle:

- If the original motivation was external, ask yourself what reward arises internally (from within the protagonist) that makes her persist. What is her personal (either conscious or unconscious) reason for acting the way she does?
- If the original motivation was internal, examine what external motivations (outside of the character) pull her up when she falls.

Also consider her motivations as they relate to the prevalent themes throughout your story. How does her motivation tie into the themes your story explores? How can you more closely tie her motivation to your story themes? (For more on theme, visit Part Three of this book.)

The deeper middle is more than an exotic world filled with antagonists, relentless conflicts, and challenges that keep the protagonist from what she wants. Yes, the dilemmas and setbacks she endures in the middle provide drama and page-turnability. However, the struggles to survive and go forward also offer gifts in the form of inner changes that will serve her well in her Triumph, when she has fully adapted her thinking to the demands of her new reality.

The deeper and more lasting point of the conflict and challenges in the deeper middle is to change and expand the protagonist. The gifts that prepare her for the ultimate confrontation at the end and reveal her full transformation are presented in the deeper middle through her interactions and relationships with other characters, both allies and antagonists.

These gifts may include the following:

- advice given
- clues shared
- lessons taught
- beliefs held
- abilities advanced
- strengths developed

Ree travels though the deeper middle with a single primary goal—to find her father. Yes, she must put food on the table and uses this need to teach her siblings how to fire a gun, ostensibly to hunt for food and, more subtly, to prepare them to defend themselves. And, yes, she is going after her father in order to keep a roof over her family's heads—a noble goal with a noble motivation. All the while, as she presses forward, every secondary character, motivated by protecting the status quo, has a primary goal of keeping Ree from discovering the truth: that her father is dead. Before she can learn the truth, the secondary characters test her loyalty and, at the same time, teach her to respect those in charge, or at least to play by their rules.

Emotion at the Dark Night

The Third Energetic Marker, Dark Night, is the lowest point of your protagonist's journey. This is a time of crisis, loss, even death. The failure or success the protagonist suffers at this turning point in the story strips away all of her defensive postures and informs us on the deepest level of who she truly is as compared to who she always thought she was and how she conveyed herself to be throughout the story.

The Dark Night of the Pulitzer Prize–winning novel *The Goldfinch* by Donna Tartt begins when the protagonist, Theo Decker, runs into his old friend Boris, a man to whom he opened up his alienated heart with the help of dangerous drugs and risky behavior during their high school years. Theo has been living a lie and torturing himself over the safety of a tiny oil painting of a goldfinch. He had stolen the painting from a museum he and his mother were visiting; during the visit, a bomb exploded, resulting in his mother's death.

Within a short time of entering the crisis scene at the Dark Night, the relative stability and sense of control Theo had painfully created in his life is destroyed as Boris reminds Theo of a past he'd much rather forget: drinking alcohol to the point of becoming sick, taking drugs, climbing the roof and jumping into the swimming pool, lying on his back on a darkened street at night and waiting for a car to run him over, trying to set the house on fire, burning the sofa. Through this behavior and under Boris's destructive influence, he came to believe that it was his fault his mother died. He also believes that if he had died as well, he "… would maybe be with her, together in the darkness …"

With the tension and sense of doom mounting, the crisis crescendos as Boris shows Theo visual proof that the treasured painting is currently in Boris's possession: "… he punched up a picture on his iPhone. Then he handed it across the table to me."

Upon seeing that the museum painting of his precious finch—the greatest reminder of and tribute to his mother—is with Boris rather than in the safe place he'd hidden it, Theo's world is turned upside down.

> The atoms in my head were spinning apart: the sparkle of the bump had already begun to turn, apprehension and disquiet moving in subtly like dark air before a thunderstorm.

This scene between Theo and Boris is a classic crisis scene in that it represents the antagonist's (Boris's) triumph. It is the point in the story when all feels lost, the darkest moment for Theo in the entire story. He has failed to keep safe that which is of ultimate importance to him.

After the Dark Night, he can never return to his shadow life and his old tendencies to pretend and deny.

The Character Confronts Her Shadow and Reclaims a Lost Part of Herself

As we noted in Part One, the scenes that follow the Dark Night markedly change in energy from those that come before. There is still a sense of urgency, but it has lulled in the quake of the Third Energetic Marker. Before the protagonist can move beyond her breakdown to find a breakthrough, first she must come to an understanding of what went wrong.

Often this breakthrough is revealed in an ensuing epiphany scene after the Dark Night scene(s). As we've said before, an epiphany scene is when something breaks open in the heart and mind of the character as she realizes her part in her own failures. She gains surprising new insight, awakens to element(s) of herself she's been oblivious to, and/or breaks through denial.

As she begins to grasp her dark or weak side, she is forced into new understandings of herself. This understanding is revealed in new and clear ways, which will directly affect choices and decisions she makes and will ultimately contribute to an emotionally fulfilling transformation at the end of the book.

Moments leading to personal growth and change deeply connect with readers. If the epiphany scene that follows the Dark Night does not show the protagonist coming to some sort of emotional awareness, your story can become stagnant and sever the reader's tie to the story. Stories are living, breathing organisms, as is the protagonist. She must grow and change as she tries to obtain something, fails, and tries again.

Each time your protagonist is knocked down, she must get back up and try again—especially now, after the greatest blow of all.

Often a series of epiphany scenes are necessary before the character can truly sort out what's happened and what part she played in the disaster, and how she can prepare to reach victory. As a result of her epiphany(s), she is forced to make a choice or a change. The epiphany should either come at a cost or renew her hope and faith and rise directly out of plot events and information—it should not come out of the blue. The knowledge, understanding, and new insights should also reflect important thematic elements.

Once she has become conscious of all that has come before, she understands the strength and courage she's gained in her suffering and the freedom it has afforded her. This new understanding will directly affect choices and decisions she makes as she moves forward.

She knows her journey is not over and that the worst awaits her. The more the protagonist knows about what's coming, the more suspense is generated and the stronger the reader's connection to her. The scenes that fall directly after the Dark Night, as she struggles to make sense of all that has happened to her, are the protagonist's time to make plans. If her plans seem illogical or misguided, readers have cause to worry. If she seems too confident in anticipation of the challenges ahead of her, the reader will worry even more—which is a good thing.

Throughout the deeper middle, emotional undercurrents and shadows appear in every scene and in other characters as the protagonist estimates what is necessary for ultimate success in achieving her goal. She gathers the attributes, objects, and people she needs for the final journey to the end. She leaves behind everything that does not serve her ultimate goal.

After Ree's Dark Night in *Winter's Bone* when she is beaten unconscious "for not listening," her uncle shows up and carries her to his truck. On the way to taking her home, he finally tells her the truth: that her daddy is dead. Afterwards, Ree "lies on her bed wafting in and out of consciousness." Later we see her with her girlfriend, "feeling worried and defeated," as she considers her siblings. Not liking her option of farming them out to family, she goes looking for money and housing from the Army recruiter at her high school and learns more bad news.

> **RECRUITER:** …once you join up, there's no turning back, and it might not be worth forty thousand dollars to you.
>
> **REE:** Well, the main reason is I need the money. It'd be nice to travel, I suppose.
>
> **RECRUITER:** You know, five years is a long commitment.
>
> **REE:** Well, how long before I get the money?
>
> **RECRUITER:** Well, after you sign up it would be anywhere between fourteen weeks to eighty-two weeks.
>
> **REE:** Well, how come it doesn't say that on the poster?
>
> **RECRUITER:** Probably a clerical error, or it just wasn't on there. It might have been in fine print at the bottom.

Knowing What She Wants, the Character Moves Toward the Light with Purpose

No matter how far she may be from her original goal, after the character awakens she begins her character arc transformation by thinking and acting differently. The moment she moves toward her long-term goal, she crosses over into the end of the story, where she begins her final ascent, the climb that's designed to get her to the right place at the right time to seize back her personal power from the antagonist.

By slowing the action and drama for one or several scenes following the Dark Night, when the energy rises to announce the final quarter, the story can now move forward quickly and with maximum impact to the final marker: the protagonist's Triumph.

Later, Ree is asleep on the couch at her house, which will soon be seized by the courts. Teardrop appears and jostles her awake with his knee.

REE: What's going on?

TEARDROP: I'm tired of waiting around for shit to come down. Let's get out and poke 'em where they're at and see what happens.

When Teardrop helps Ree up off the couch and they drive off in his truck, the final quarter and end of the story begins.

IN SUMMARY

Throughout the deeper middle of the story:

- the protagonist gets a taste of her integrated self and what it means to her story.
- her longing and goal appear to be within reach.
- around three-quarters of the way into the story, the Dark Night arrives. At this juncture, the character's shadow still has power, and she suffers a great loss as a result of blind action.
- the character confronts her shadow and reclaims a lost part of herself.
- the character moves toward her goal with purpose and self-awareness.

CHAPTER ELEVEN

EMOTION IN THE END SCENES

Integration Is Complete

Scene types addressed: climax scenes, final scenes, resolution scenes, romance scenes, suspense scenes, twister scenes, triumph scenes

EMOTION IN THE END

The end is an exhilarating place for writer, reader, and protagonist, for this is where your protagonist at last becomes victorious in one way or another, where her shadow is fully integrated, and where she gets to revel in the light of her strengths as well as bask in the pleasure of achieving her goals in one form or another. It's not without cost or suffering—in fact, she has most likely suffered a great deal by now—but your end scenes are where you give back to your character all that she has lost and perhaps more. Her inner world will demonstrate growth and maturity.

Here she will undergo her Triumph—the high point of her story and the apex of her transformation or acquisition of goals; for the antagonist, however, it is the lowest point, often resulting in his complete vanquishing.

All of this awareness and the ensuing confrontation will happen very quickly, however. Your final scenes comprise about one-quarter of your entire book, much like your beginning.

The Character Sees Herself Clearly and Reaches Self-Understanding

A hallmark of emotional maturity is when a character can see himself, his flaws, and his strengths with clarity. While his flaws are not completely overcome, they have been transformed into useful tools and resources that the now-integrated protagonist can use for his own growth and the growth of others around him.

In Patry Francis's layered psychological novel, *The Orphans of Race Point*, protagonist Hallie Costa begins the novel as a motherless child who befriends another motherless boy, co-protagonist Gus. Hallie wants two things: to feel a sense of family that her mother's death deprived her of, and to follow in her father's footsteps to study medicine. Hallie's and Gus's love seems fated from early on when Hallie helps Gus through the aftermath of his mother's murder at the hand of his rage-prone, alcoholic father.

Indeed, as teens they fall in love and become a couple. Hallie is determined that she and Gus will entwine their lives, despite her father's insistence that she follow her own path. But when a terrible accident changes everything between her and Gus at the story's Point of No Return, her life veers off course, and it takes years for her to find her footing again.

Gus, meanwhile, turns away from his familiar life, rejects romantic love (and thus Hallie), and becomes a priest. Years later, he becomes caught up in the domestic drama of a woman named Ava and is then indicted for her murder. Hallie, who is now a doctor and is married to a man with whom she is not passionately in love, does not believe Gus is guilty. She returns to Provincetown to help prove his innocence. Her only real hope in this endeavor is to find the daughter of the murdered woman, Mila, who was home the night her mother was killed. Hallie experiences her Dark Night when Gus, reacting to a prison rape, nearly kills his aggressor, thereby damaging Hallie's attempt to win his freedom. In her stress, Hallie miscarries, realizes she is not in love with her husband, and believes Gus's freedom to be lost, as well.

Deprived of a nuclear family because of her mother's death, unable to create the family she wanted with Gus, and facing the failure of her marriage, by the end of the novel, through many trials and revelations, Hallie has cobbled together her own version of a family of "orphans" as she heals her emotional wounds. She has come to see that in lieu of the family she thinks she wants, she can create one even more deeply satisfying. Her new family consists of teenaged Mila, the orphaned daughter of the woman Gus was accused of murdering; Lunes Oliveras, the lawyer who originally represented Gus; and other friends who have known Hallie and Gus in the Provincetown community where they all grew up. Together Hallie and her family piece together the truth of what really happened at The Triumph—which leads to Gus's freedom from jail and Hallie's freedom from the illusions of immature love and into a mature reality of what family and love mean to her.

No matter how happy the ending you prepare for your protagonist, it has to be earned. Often your character finds a new kind of happiness at the end of his story, one he could never have envisioned at the beginning because he was still bound by the confines of his shadow world. This is important to consider when you're writing your way to the end—don't become too attached to a particular outcome. In many cases, you can't even know the true beginning of your story until you've written the ending. The ending has to be true to your character's goals and desires; it has to be true to how and why he overcomes his flaws; it has to be authentic and reflect where he began.

The Character Understands the Purpose of Her Antagonists

So how do you get your protagonist to this place of integration and healing? In this final quarter of your story, you must remove all remaining blinders from your protagonist's eyes and heart. You must strip any last illusions the protagonist clung to through the Dark Night, and this will make her stronger and more emotionally resilient and empowered, even if she must endure one last shock of understanding or painful revelation at the Triumph. More important, what gives her the power to rise above her antagonists is that she has integrated her shadow—her wounds, her flaws, her sense of injustice or blame—and has become a whole person. The flaws that held her back before now serve a purpose in her life—she understands how they have led her to be the person she is. She can now rise above old behaviors and attitudes (unlike antagonists, who often don't see their fatal flaws until it is far too late, causing their downfall).

Sarah Waters's epic historical novel, *Fingersmith*, is a page-turning novel full of twister, revelation, and epiphany scenes, and is a marvelous study for any writer who wants to keep readers on their toes. Through the use of powerful antagonists in the form of people, the time period (nineteenth-century London), and the protagonist's inner demons, Waters sets up a protagonist whose transformation by the end of the novel is nothing short of miraculous.

Protagonist Sue Trinder has been born and raised in little more than a den of thieves in 1800s London. Hers is a life of pickpocketing and graft; she is one of many orphans raised by the noble Mrs. Sucksby. But Sue's fate, unbeknownst to her, has been part of a very long scheme, which culminates in the months before her eighteenth birthday. Under the pretense of suckering an innocent, housebound, wealthy young lady named Maud to marry "Gentleman"—a friend of Mrs. Sucksby's—so that he can claim Maud's money, have her committed, and share the spoils with Sue's den of thieves, Sue is established to become Maud's new maid and help carry out the scheme.

Throughout the middle, a series of shocking revelations not only cracks open Sue's careful, stealthy life in the shadows but also turns her emotions in myriad directions by completely twisting her goals and desires as antagonists change the story. Sue has lived an isolated, small life in her London home. In the first revelation in the deeper middle, she realizes she is falling in love with Maud. This, in and of itself, is a serious emotional drama for Sue, as during this time period there were no open lesbians; if anything, such an attraction would have been considered a sin of perversion that could cost her everything. Still, she knows what she feels is love, and this causes her to question the morality of the grift being played against Maud. The situation is further complicated when Maud seems to express feelings of love in return.

Waters twists the emotional plot by causing the reader to wonder if Sue will be able to go against her feelings in order to carry out the scheme. She then pushes the emotional intensity even further by invoking a twister scene at Sue's Dark Night. When Sue learns, on the night of Gentleman's marriage to Maud, that *Sue* is the real victim of Gentleman's scheme, and that Maud was not innocent at all but working with him to trap her, she is horrified and betrayed. Sue, not Maud, is presented to the doctors of an asylum as the "mad" Mrs. Rivers, Gentlemen's allegedly addled wife.

> There was a second, I think, of perfect stillness. I looked at him, and he nodded. "Mrs Rivers?" he said again. Then Gentleman leaned and caught hold of my arm. I thought at first he meant to keep me in my seat; then I understood that he was trying to press me from it. The doctor took my other arm. They got me to my feet. My shoes caught upon the steps, I said,
>
> "Wait! What are you doing? What—?"

At first, Sue fights their grip, swearing and struggling. Then shock settles in, and we see her sink into the despair of this twist. To add insult to her sense of betrayal, she is then locked in a brutal women's institution in an era where women were placed there for life. Waters plants us firmly inside Sue's experience through sensory details of the asylum—we are right there with her in her horror, her shock, her dismay, and, of course, her terror at what her future will bring. This twister scene sets us up for her eventual Triumph, which will be all that much more victorious when she gets her revenge.

Emotion in the Buildup to the Triumph

Remember that before the Triumph Energetic Marker, the protagonist spends a couple of "buildup" scenes gathering forces and resources, both inner and outer, and preparing himself for what is to come. Here Sue undergoes great emotional upheavals while locked in the women's asylum. "Cures" resemble torture, and the nurses, who have little supervision, take pleasure in tormenting and beating their mad charges, making Sue's life a living hell. To survive, she marshals deep inner steel, mostly by cultivating her anger at those who betrayed her. She is determined to keep her brain alert by finding an escape, all the while surviving in a place that is meant to break and subdue its residents.

Whereas early in the novel Sue behaved as a pawn of others and did as she was told with blind obedience, now she has endured so much that she pushes back against the literal confines of her environment and antagonists. And as she finds her inner steel, a break comes in the action of her plot.

She receives a visit from Charles, the knife-sharpening boy she knew at the mansion where she'd played the part of Maud's dutiful maid. Charles doesn't realize that Sue was put into the asylum instead of Maud, and he comes to the asylum seeking to speak to Maud. He is attempting to track down the missing Gentleman because he wants to leave his miserable life behind and work with him, not realizing that Gentleman is the purveyor of the terrible grift against Sue.

> Charles looked me over as I have said; then he tilted his head and looked past me, and past Nurse Spiller, as if he thought that Maud must be coming along. Then he looked at me again, and his eyes grew wide.
>
> And it was that, that saved me. His were the first two eyes, in all the time that had passed since I left Mrs Cream's, that had looked at me and seen, not Maud, but Sue.

In the buildup to the Triumph, your character must show emotional resolve, courage, and determination, qualities he has earned through the trials he has experienced throughout the story. He may surprise himself here, discovering he is a tougher, wiser, kinder person than he realized in the beginning scenes.

The following scene types will be most useful to you at this stage of the game.

Twister Scenes

Remember that a twister scene is a suspenseful scene that turns the dramatic action plot on its head, rerouting where both reader and protagonist believed they were heading. In the character's emotional landscape, shock or surprise present itself again and again, and often the protagonist is left with a feeling of having acted or been played for the fool, and having been blind to the truth before her. But as we get to the end of the novel, twisters can bring a sense of emotional relief, turning the stakes in her favor as the truth now empowers and emboldens her.

The buildup to Sue's triumph begins when she manages, in yet another twister scene, to escape from her asylum with Charles's help. (You might say this whole novel is a study in the masterful use of the twister scene.)

Armed with the knowledge of her antagonists' identities and their true motivations, Sue makes her way back home, where she plans to reveal Gentleman's diabolical betrayal to Mrs. Sucksby and take her revenge.

When she returns "home," the following scene brings shocking revelations and high suspense when she finds Maud in her place acting as her. From here, the whole story unravels.

> I looked again at Maud—at her neat ear which, I now saw, had a crystal drop falling from it on a wire of gold; and at the curls in her fair hair; and at her dark eye-brows. They had been tweezered into two fine arches. …
>
> I felt tears rise into my throat.
>
> "You have taken everything that was mine," I said. "You have taken it, and made it better."

"I took it," she answered, "*because* it was yours. Because I must!"

"Why must you? Why?"

She opened her mouth to speak. Then she looked at Mrs Sucksby and her face changed.

"For villainy's sake," she said flatly. "For villainy's sake. Because you were right, before: my face is a false one, my mouth is an actress mouth, my blushes tell lies, my eyes—My eyes—" She looked away. Her voice had begun to rise. She made it flat again. "Richard found that, after all, we must wait for our money, longer than we thought."

Suspense Scenes

The most versatile scene type at this stage of your story is a suspense scene. Remember that suspense scenes create apprehension and anxiety in both the reader and the protagonist. Their medium is uncertainty: We don't know what's going to happen next, we sense physical and/or emotional danger, and we can't put down the book until we know how the events shake out. These scenes work especially well when we are deeply inside the protagonist's experience through the use of sensory description; brief, tense thoughts; and close POV, in which the reader can see and know only as much as the character does. Omniscient point of view, in which the reader, through a "god-like" lens, sees and knows all, can actually drain away suspense because it gives away too much.

At the buildup to the Triumph, the reader is waiting to see if the protagonist has truly changed, grown, and earned his emotional maturity. In the end scenes, especially after a twister, you want to keep suspense high, never letting it drop until the Triumph has peaked.

Emotion at the Triumph

We now arrive at the Triumph marker, comprised of one or several scenes that build to the major climax of the story's emotional and action plots. This is where your protagonist will earn her victory and achieve emotional fulfillment of some kind. However, it may be a hard-won victory, a victory with a cost. Vanquishing antagonists is no small feat, and there is often fallout, such as regret that the antagonist didn't back down when he could, or melancholy over what once was.

In *Fingersmith*, if the Dark Night was the lowest point for Sue because everything she knew and felt turned out to be a lie, her Triumph begins when she returns home to Mrs. Sucksby's after her escape from the asylum, brandishing the truth as a weapon. Little does Sue know that she has changed so much that Mrs. Sucksby's doesn't feel like home any more—but that's a good thing. By the end of the novel your protagonist should be able to see her shadow life for what it was, and it should no longer fit the person she has become.

The relief of being home sharply contrasts for Sue with the discovery of Maud aligned with Mrs. Sucksby. It means that everyone, even her beloved mother figure, has betrayed her.

Dialogue Scenes

Waters now turns to dialogue—interwoven with high suspense—to reveal the remaining details that there simply isn't time to reveal in any other way: Sue learns that all her "family" and friends have been complicit in this betrayal her whole life. All those she has loved have turned out to be antagonists, and her life has been a lie built upon others' greed.

Though in this section we are discussing emotion in the end scenes, in many novels, the end scenes move so fast, and focus so much on the action, that emotion is conveyed mostly in the emboldened way the protagonist acts. Dialogue scenes, which move with an illusion of real time, often feel like action, and yet you can still charge them full of emotion. Because your protagonist has changed internally, he now draws upon his new internal wellspring of emotional strength to speak with determination and power.

You'll be using twister, suspense, and dialogue scenes in the buildup to the Triumph Energetic Marker, which usually relies on one or more climax scenes. Also, a note: The buildup is rarely a time for slow, quiet contemplation (other than perhaps a small "pep talk" the protagonist gives himself before launching into the fray). Save musings and reflection for the resolution after the Triumph.

Climax Scenes

The word *climax* is loaded for many reasons, but it suggests a steadily building, upward momentum and energy, both internally in the emotional realm and externally in the dramatic action. In *Fingersmith*, once Sue returns home, the truth unravels quickly, beat after beat. Gentleman unwittingly shows up, unaware that Sue has escaped. Sue has finally mustered the courage to face the people who have lied to her and betrayed her, and she demands answers from everyone. When the answers reveal more painful truths, Sue turns her hurt and outrage on Gentleman, whom she sees as the cause of all her misery. A scuffle ensues, and, in the climax of the scene, Gentleman is stabbed.

In the aftermath of the tragedy, Mrs. Sucksby, aware that she is responsible in many ways for all this emotional suffering and the subsequent physical chaos, reveals one last crucial secret that, though painful, sets Sue free to claim her true self. In fact, it is the first time in Sue's life that she gets to live fully in the light, not only because she knows her real origins and name, and can make an honest life that's not built on thievery and lies, but also so she can claim the love that is forbidden her by her society and times, whether she and Maud ever reunite or she simply moves on to find it elsewhere.

The Character Is Victorious in Integrating the Shadow

As we've noted throughout this book, your character is continually progressing out of the shadows and away from his own shadow, into the light of healing, wholeness, and integration. Emotionally the concept of the shadow refers to your protagonist's darkness, lack of awareness, and flaws. Just like Wendy must sew Peter Pan's shadow back onto him before he can be whole, in your story, your character must embrace and understand his own darkness by the end so that he will not be doomed to repeat his errors.

Returning to *The Orphans of Race Point*, at the end of the novel Hallie finally understands herself and her shadow, has made meaning of all her trials, and sees clearly why she was so obsessively drawn to Gus—both orphaned of their mothers at a young age, her grief matched his and drew her into his world of emotional volatility. She wanted love, but she was seeking a wounded love, not a mature love. By the end, she has not only healed but understands why everyone acted as they did, and she can forgive. Amidst some of the more bittersweet moments is a feeling that Hallie now knows what kind of love she really needs as an adult who has been through more than a few romantic battles, and she will seek it out and accept it when she finds it. She has learned that the love she had for Gus when they were kids was an immature love, a love borne of need and trauma—and while it shaped both of them, and contributed powerfully to their development, they can't go back in time and re-create what never existed in the first place (though they will always be friends). We end with both characters choosing growth and wholeness over youthful passion, a choice that promises a new, more hopeful future.

> As she closed the book, she remembered Gus's long silence ... and the calmness of his voice when he finally spoke; and she knew, with absolute certainty, that whatever curses Gus had endured, his gift was far greater. ... She could never have imagined how his grief would infiltrate her life. But even if she had known, she would not have turned back.

Romance and Sex in the End Scenes

Many books that don't fall into the romance genre nonetheless contain a romantic emotional plot of some kind: love and deep friendship that buds early and takes the course of the story to fulfill its journey. And, just in case you weren't sure, a romantic interest doesn't turn a book into a romance novel; in fact, the story is not a romance so long as there is more going on than just the acquisition of said romantic partner.

After the Triumph, many books use resolution and even final scenes to bring the protagonist together with her love interest, whether simply to reunite them or to consummate their relationship at last. When two characters finally get to be together after spending the course of a story dancing at each other's edges or slipping through each other's grasp, it grants the reader much-earned satisfaction. In that way, stories reflect what we want for our own lives.

If your character is in romantic pursuit, at the end it's likely she will achieve emotional fulfillment in a relationship and will possibly even make love. But because we are now at the point of integration, be sure your protagonist is not settling for scraps or begging for attention. This may also be where she abandons the notion she had of one kind of love, or even one person, only to take up with the version or person that now aligns with who she has become. Now she brings herself as a complete person to this relationship. If they make love, she does so with eyes open and full consent. If they agree to be together, it is a mature choice.

IN SUMMARY

At the end of your story, your protagonist acts with more emotional maturity and courage than he has in any section, often for the first time. His suffering in the middle was necessary, and it is at the end that he understands, and integrates, the reasons why. The end scenes are the proving ground for the protagonist to demonstrate changed behavior and beliefs. After the Triumph, you move into resolution scenes (unless you are creating a cliff-hanger for a sequel in a series, in which case you have more room to leave action and emotional plots open). In the resolution phase, you have the chance to depict romantic and sexual consummation.

In the end scenes:

- show how the character now influences the action through his new strength, determination, and maturity.

- show how the action leads to the protagonist's transformed emotional maturity.
- show how the protagonist demonstrates internal changes through new strategies and actions learned throughout the middle of the story.
- show how relationships may be gained or consummated at the end, and how those relationships align with the protagonist's new emotional maturity.

Part Three

THEME

CHAPTER TWELVE

THEME IN THE BEGINNING SCENES

Wading Through the Shadows

Scene types discussed: first scenes, suspense scenes

Every story has a unique set of themes and meanings. If action is the clock of your plot, and emotion is the layer that touches people's hearts, then theme is the link that connects both elements and creates a greater sense of significance. No matter what scene type you use, always pull in thematic elements to deepen and enrich your story. Even when you don't plant them consciously, they will turn up and readers will interpret their own meaning. Better to be in control of where and how these thematic elements are placed.

Theme enhances the emotional impact on characters and readers alike and conveys a feeling that your plot's action has greater purpose. With a strong theme, your story resonates with the reader long after she puts it down. When we think theme, we tend to think in loaded words like *loyalty*, *forgiveness*, and *redemption*, but these words are just touchstones that carry within them entire galaxies of subthemes and concepts that relate to your plot. Within *loyalty*, for instance, you may find *family*, *love*, *truth*, *honesty*, and so on. Within *redemption* you may find threads of *betrayal* and *life purpose*.

While some writers know their story's theme before they ever set out to write, and some even create each scene with an overarching thematic goal, most are driven by love of characters or action, or just a fascination with the worlds they create. Often it isn't until much later in the process that they begin to look at what their stories are really about, and whether the book holds together beneath that important concept. In fact, though you may have a cursory idea of your theme, you won't be able to fully integrate thematic elements into your whole story until you've finished at least one draft.

Theme is another lens through which to look at your story. Check to see if certain scenes or sections are not working toward the thematic whole. In this chapter, we will explore several ways to tip off the reader to your story's theme.

CONVEYING THEME THROUGH IMAGES OR SYMBOLS

An image is a description of anything that can be seen or felt (drawing on the senses) in your work. However, images are also stylized descriptions selected to evoke emotional, symbolic, and further meanings for the reader.

At their most basic, powerful images are dressed-up figures of speech such as similes and metaphors. In a simile, a thing or person is compared to another thing or person, and becomes more powerful or enhanced by comparison. Here is an example of a metaphor from Rene Denfeld's novel *The Enchanted*: "… the consonants grow into planets that become the universe …". In a metaphor, a thing or a person is described as being another thing. Here is another metaphor from Katherine Dunn's novel *Geek Love*: "This fragile flammable heap is all that's left of my life." Well-placed and carefully crafted similes and metaphors can add profound depth and can convey so much more than a straightforward description.

Images are the most evocative way to draw the reader's attention to the theme of the story in a subtle way. They are incredibly useful when you want to point the reader's attention to the theme (or themes) of your story without getting out a banner that shrieks "Forgiveness and Redemption!"

Maybe you'd like to avoid being overly sentimental about the fact that an abusive mother and her cowed daughter have made peace. So in the background of a scene in which they are having their first cup of coffee together in years, you avoid the maudlin description of the mother clasping the daughter's head to her breast and instead plant an image. You might write, for example: "Just beyond my mother's head, the moth that had been struggling in the spider web broke free and flitted like a white flag before perching to rest on the windowsill."

The theme of forgiveness, as evidenced in the white flag and the moth breaking free, will spill delicately into the reader's subconscious.

While images lean away from the literal and more toward the poetic realm of analogy, symbols or talismans are actual *things*—objects, mostly, and occasionally people—that represent the meaning of your story and can be planted within it. Earlier in this book we used examples from Marisha Pessl's dark thriller *Night Film*. In it, the antagonist, Cordova, is an occult filmmaker who uses a very specific shot of an eye, in close-up, as his signature image in every film. It's described by an interviewer as "sovereign, deadly, perfect" and represents the theme of evil the filmmaker seeks to explore in his films. But it also works as a metaphor for the protagonist's pursuit of evil, which the interviewer believes resides in Cordova. The eye, then, is both a literal thing and a symbol—it represents the clarity and truth seeking that drives the action and emotion of the novel. The protagonist, Scott McGrath, ruthlessly hunts the truth, while Cordova fiercely protects his own truth behind a veil of symbolic imagery. When the eye appears, we're being asked to remember that this is a book about two very different versions of what can be seen and known. Pessl plants it at the beginning of the novel but then recalls it throughout the story as a kind of talisman, or symbolic object, constantly reminding the reader that things may not be what they seem.

In other novels a simple item—a doll, a journal, a mother's locket, a ring—may act as a symbol that plays powerfully on the theme. When the object appears, the writer is often pointing us toward thematic significance, and this is a powerful way for you to do the same.

While we're on the subject of imagery, let's go a little further into it, because crafting effective imagery is one of the most powerful methods for subtly demonstrating the themes that will resonate deeply with your readers.

Using Images

It can take a while to understand what we mean by the word *image*—but let the word itself be a guide. When you create an image, you are painting a picture, a visual, in the reader's mind. This is different from, say, dialogue, which is "spoken" into a reader's inner ear, or descriptions of actions, which state what happens and how. An image could neatly be translated to film. Images often stick in a reader's memory because they have symbolic potency, and they are a wonderful method for steering clear of summary and exposition that gets in the way of your story. Here's how to craft one.

Demonstrate an Aspect of Your Character or Narrator

If you struggle with the urge to "tell" characters into being, images will help you use metaphor to avoid that bad habit. Rather than calling a character "stubborn," you could write: "The way he held his ground reminded me of the fat, black lab my daddy had; he growled if you tried to make him go for a walk and bared his yellow teeth if you so much as breathed near his food bowl."

Yes, the visual is describing a dog, not your character, but it does the trick—the two are now equated, and merged, in the reader's mind.

Evoke Emotion Without Exposition

Let's say, for example, you want the reader to know that your character or narrator is in great pain or shock, but you want readers to *feel* this deeply in their heart and body, not just in their mind. You don't want to write, "It pained him to see his father so weak and sickly." Readers won't have an emotional experience—they'll be passive witnesses.

But what happens when you write, "His father's limbs looked tough and dry, like cords of tanned leather his grandpa used to hang on the porch," or "In place of the barrel-chested mammoth of a man was a frail specimen, like a pale, bald runt of the litter whose fate was to be drowned …"? By comparing an ailing father's limbs to dried leather or to a bald runt that must be drowned, the effect you create gets the reader a lot closer to an emotional experience.

Foreshadow Future Plot or Story Elements

Imagine you've written a story in which someone is murdered by being bludgeoned with a candlestick. Let's say you want to drop a hint to the reader at some point about the manner of the person's death, inserting a clue without saying it outright, to build suspense. You might create an image that compares a candlestick to something else—maybe something benign, even, to deflect the reader.

For example: "The candle and its flame reminded him of a field of pink tulips, slender stems balancing improbably heavy heads."

Zoom the Reader's Eye in Close at the Beginning or the End of a Scene

Employing a strong image is a powerful way to begin or end a scene. An image can stand in for a more dramatic epiphany or cliff-hanger. This is how Janet Fitch's novel *White Oleander* (which is rife with great imagery!) begins.

> The Santa Anas blew in hot from the desert, shriveling the last of the
> spring grass into whiskers of pale straw. Only the oleanders thrived,
> their delicate poisonous blooms, their dagger green leaves.

The narrator's fate is very much linked to these poisonous blooms, so
using "dagger green leaves" and the imagery of a hot, scorching wind
in the beginning of the book is not only compelling and beautiful but
thematically purposeful. We are made to understand from the beginning that something deadly is about to unfold.

Similarly you can end a scene on a haunting or powerful image, like
this one from Amy Hempel's *Tumble Home*.

> The tide this time of year washes hundreds of tiny starfish up onto the
> beach. It leaves them stranded in salty constellations, a sandy galaxy
> within reach.

The image speaks powerfully to the complex nature of relationships, as
water is always a stand-in for emotion.

INTRODUCING THEME IN THE FIRST SCENE

Thematic elements reflect where your protagonist is at every stage of the
novel. These are the little touches that speak to the reader's subconscious.
At the beginning, your character lives in the shadow realm, and goals
and adventure have yet to change her. Your thematic imagery, therefore, must reflect this level of her awareness and stage of her journey.
Remember that beginning scenes also need to steer clear of too much
exposition or explanatory language. The theme is only being introduced.
Also avoid heavy-handed statements such as "This is a story about love."

In Gillian Flynn's psychological thriller *Sharp Objects*, protagonist
Libby Day is an orphan. Her only living relative is her brother, who is
in jail for the murder of the rest of her family. Her father disappeared
when she was young and is possibly dead. Now in her twenties, she
doesn't have many memories from the night of the murders that took
place when she was a small child, and she's been living on the proceeds

of donations made on her behalf over the years by well-wishers who felt bad for her in the wake of the tragedy. She believes in her own essential badness, not because she has done anything bad, but because she thinks she is corrupt right down to her blood—an evil she inherited, perhaps. Libby begins her story, in the first scene, in a dark emotional place. Notice the images Flynn uses to describe Libby.

> I have a meanness inside me, real as an organ. Slit me at my belly and it might slide out, meaty and dark, drop on the floor so you could stomp on it. It's the Day blood. Something's wrong with it.

We have *slit* and *belly*, *organ* and *meat*, *dark* and *drop*—all words that conjure visceral images about the body, death, and horror—words that slide out to create thematic symbolism reflecting the slaughter of her family. These image words do an interesting job here in the first scene: (a) They invoke the horror of what happened to Libby's family (and, indirectly, to her) without telling us a single backstory detail, and (b) they plant a seed of uncertainty in the reader about this character. It's not a seed that makes us want to run away but rather one that creates curiosity. We want to find out if this girl is as bad as she says she is. We hope to learn the truth about her family's tragic end. We root for her to get out of her dark place. Ultimately this is very much a book about the bonds of blood—of what ties, and what breaks, a family apart, and how people do, or don't, put themselves back together.

Libby doesn't stop there. As the scene progresses, the imagery stays firmly planted in the realm of viscera.

> I can feel a better version of me somewhere in there—hidden behind a liver or attached to a bit of spleen within my stunted, childish body—a Libby that's telling me to get up, do something, grow up, move on. But the meanness usually wins out. My brother slaughtered my family when I was seven. My mom, two sisters, gone: bang, bang, chop chop, choke choke.

Flynn's use of bodily images is emotionally and physically evocative. It brings home the reality of what murder really means: the loss of a physical presence on the earth. The loss of a mother to take the protagonist in her arms; the loss of sisters to play and braid hair with. The imagery provides a stark reminder of what murder steals. But Libby also gives us a hint of the potential hidden within this "mean" and "stunted girl"— there's hope for Libby after all, "hidden behind a liver"—which suggests that Libby must learn to identify and find her own inner essential goodness. This is a character for whom the reader hopes the story will offer transformation and redemption.

HANDLING THEME IN THE SHADOW WORLD OF THE BEGINNING SCENES

In addition to your first scene, you will have several scenes in the beginning that set up the first quarter of your book and reveal your character in his shadow world. These early scenes are all about the shadow realm—vices and secrets, flaws and bad behavior, nightmares and trauma, wounds and pressure. Your character may not literally live in a dark or shadowy place or even with shadowy characters; people in his life may seem perfectly nice and normal to him. However, the character should either have a seed of dissatisfaction about his current lot in life or be subjected to a change that will wrench him out of his cocoon.

Every protagonist's shadow realm is different. Lionel Essrog, in Jonathan Lethem's *Motherless Brooklyn*, was raised in foster care and now works as a young adult for a mobster who runs a shady private detective business. His Tourette's syndrome is as much a part of his shadow world as are the literally shadowy alleyways and corners where he often finds himself squatting and waiting to acquire information.

The beginning scenes of Lethem's novel make wonderful use of language-based images that show Lionel's struggles with his disorder. At this early stage of the game, he is still ashamed of himself, still letting others consider him "a freak."

> My mouth won't quit, though mostly I whisper or subvocalize like
> I'm reading aloud, my Adam's apple bobbing, jaw muscle beating like
> a miniature heart under my cheek, the noise suppressed, the words
> escaping silently, mere ghosts of themselves, husks empty of breath
> and tone.

The novel's theme, reflected both in Lionel's struggle with his Tourette's and in the life he has found himself in, is one of learning to claim his voice, speak up for himself, and move out of the shadows of shame and powerlessness. Lethem masterfully uses the imagery of the setting to convey Lionel's powerlessness at the beginning.

> We were putting a stakeout on 109 East Eighty-fourth Street, a lone
> town house pinned between giant doorman apartment buildings, in
> and out of the foyers of which bicycle deliverymen with bags of hot
> Chinese flitted like tired moths in the fading November light.

CONVEYING THEME THROUGH CHARACTER DIALOGUE AND NARRATIVE VOICE

It's not uncommon for a character to voice the theme early on in the story in a succinct line of dialogue or narrative that resonates powerfully for the remainder of the story.

In Rene Denfeld's novel *The Enchanted*, about the people who live and interact with the death row inmates in a prison, "The Lady"—who interviews the death row inmates in an effort to save them from execution, strikes up a friendship with "The Priest." After discussing the fate of one particularly tough death row inmate, she says to him:

> "There is too much pain in the world, that's the problem."
>   "Pain and beauty, and beauty in the pain." His voice is a whisper
> that strokes her.

The novel churns with such thematic declarations as its characters grapple with what it means to be good or evil, whether one can find beauty in suffering, and whether those who have committed atrocious acts can redeem themselves. Without giving away its ending, this thematic significance, about learning to find beauty in pain, is crucial to the fate of all the characters.

In fact, the opening line is delivered in the narrative voice of a death row inmate who lives deep in the bowels of the old prison. He narrates: "This is an enchanted place. Others don't see it, but I do."

That's not what one would expect a prisoner to feel about his place of penance. Yet, from this moment on, Denfeld leads us to understand the novel's most important theme: how people survive horror with their humanity intact.

When theme comes in the form of dialogue, you want it to be memorable and potent, but you don't want it to seem heavy-handed. You want it to feel organic to the story, and to reflect, if possible, where your protagonist is in her journey. So if your theme is "love conquers all," then what piece of that statement is true at the beginning of your character's story? Perhaps it shows up in the form of longing. You could write the following.

> "If only I knew love," she told her friend, "I'd be powerful enough to do anything."

Katherine Dunn's darkly comic novel *Geek Love*, about a failing family circus that resorts to extreme measures to create its own circus of "freaks," also relies on thematic elements in dialogue. Oly, the hunchback albino dwarf, who is not considered "freak" enough by her family to be a great attraction, has grown up in a world where being abnormal is preferred to being normal. As such, she has a vastly different philosophy on the "norms" they encounter between shows.

I get glimpses of the horror of normalcy. Each of these innocents on the street is engulfed by a terror of their own ordinariness. They would do anything to be unique.

Dunn uses her characters' dialogue to ask the question "What is truly normal or abnormal?" and leads the reader to consider how twisted cultural attitudes toward normalcy often are. Here's an exchange between Oly, the albino dwarf, and her now-grown daughter, Miranda, who doesn't know that Oly is her biological mother. Miranda starts the conversation with a question.

> "What I'm asking is, am I crazy to have this liking for my tail? …You must have wished a million times to be normal."
> "No."
> "No?"
> "I've wished I had two heads. Or that I was invisible. I've wished for a fish's tail instead of legs. I've wished to be more special."
> "Not normal?"
> "Never!"

FINDING YOUR THEME AND SUBTHEMES

Think of your theme as a large umbrella that encapsulates many smaller subthemes beneath it. Your big, overarching theme may be "the power of love." Within that, however, are dozens of "themelets" or subthemes: "the need for self-love before loving another," "learning to recognize the difference between conditional and unconditional love," "the love between parents and children," "romantic versus sexual love," and so on. Just keep in mind that you are more likely to identify your subthemes first, and it may take longer to figure out how these add up to a unified overarching theme.

In the beginning scenes, you're only nodding to and planting the suggestion of theme deep in the reader's psyche, like tucking a tiny gem into a pocket. Your theme at this point will be embryonic, a suggestion, a hint. You're only beginning to introduce us to the world of the character and his problem. But the most powerful stories *do* get the theme across in the first quarter, if not in every scene of a story.

The more you learn to use imagery and careful dialogue to plant suggestions of theme throughout, the more successful you will be at building a story that rings with meaning long after the reader is finished.

There are many different approaches to helping you find your theme if you aren't certain, but a really fun, visual way to do it—especially if you already have a complete draft—is to get a set of colored highlighters and go through your manuscript, highlighting thematic elements that appear. These elements can manifest in the following ways:

- **SYMBOLS:** objects, talismans, and even people that represent an element, are metaphoric, and that speak to the subconscious rather than directly.
- **ANALOGY IMAGES OR SIMILES:** comparing something or someone to something else.
- **VISUAL IMAGES:** descriptive visuals that employ the senses.
- **DIALOGUE:** thematic elements that appear in characters' spoken dialogue.
- **NARRATIVE VOICE:** thematic elements that appear in the character's thoughts or observations (not dialogue).

Go through each chapter in which your protagonist appears, and highlight these items. After you finish, you can list on a separate sheet of paper each image you found, or you can simply scan through your highlights and see what thematic words spring to mind. Try to do a few chapters at the beginning, a few in each part of the middle, and a few chapters at the end; you should see your subthemes spring up again and again.

Whether you make lists or brainstorm bubbles, use a spreadsheet on a computer, or scribble your notes by hand, you'll start to see patterns emerge. Group the subthemes and then study this list to determine the umbrella theme that encapsulates them.

IN SUMMARY

- Often theme isn't clear until you've finished a first draft.
- Theme is best introduced in beginning scenes through imagery: analogies, metaphors, symbols, and talismans.
- Images are stylized, emotionally evocative, symbolic descriptions that provide context and feeling that deepen every scene.
- Theme can be conveyed in dialogue and narrative voice, but you must take a subtle approach, not a heavy-handed one.
- In the beginning scenes, imagery reflects your character's position in her shadow world. Use thematic elements to show fear, hurt, wounds, uncertainty, or longing.
- Learn to use imagery to build theme organically into every scene.
- When stuck on finding your theme, investigate your draft to see what thematic elements are already present.

CHAPTER THIRTEEN

THEME IN THE EMERGING MIDDLE SCENES

The Great Unknown

Scene types addressed: contemplative scenes, escape scenes, transition scenes, dialogue scenes

The middle of every story is designed primarily for the character to stumble and learn as she takes steps toward awareness and begins to separate and redefine what she pursues. In the deeper middle, discussed more in the next chapter, the protagonist becomes entangled, trapped, and ensnared in her shadow side before she is able to free herself.

Each time the protagonist is tripped up, either by antagonists or her own shadow, and she rises by moving forward again, the result is powerful meaning for the story. This theme of resilience and perseverance resonates in unique and universal ways.

When you have a strong sense of the themes and significance of your individual story, suddenly the action in the middle, the pressure from antagonists, and all the setbacks add up to a meaning deeper than the scenes themselves. One way to reinforce and support this profundity in the middle is with the use of imagery, symbols, metaphors, and settings that tease out the thematic elements and lead to understanding. These thematic elements bring wisdom to your story and cohesion to the individual scenes, even as some elements are so deeply buried that the reader may never connect to what you've done on a conscious level.

The details in a story, and even details purposely left out, foreshadow what's coming and inform the reader how to feel and relate to what is happening to the character and her world. Every bit of dialogue, seemingly random thought, song, dream, person, animal, object, and even metaphor and simile sends a message to the reader. Choosing just the right words and details when revising your story impacts the way readers later think about your book.

LIST YOUR THEMES

At the end of chapter twelve, we asked you to highlight thematic imagery in your completed manuscript.

Now go back and examine the elements you highlighted, looking for specific themes that travel in the story from the beginning all the way to the end.

For example, in the emerging middle of *Winter's Bone*, Ree's uncle tosses around his pistol during an early exchange where he warns Ree to stay home. In a story, a gun is never introduced lightly and always points to darkness.

Later, Ree teaches her siblings how to shoot a hunting rifle. Though she is using the rifle to kill food for her family's dinner that night, the appearance of another gun, this time handled by Ree, serves to heighten the violence and death that comes later in the story.

In your own manuscript, make a list of the general themes and abstract meanings that have popped up in your story and are reflected throughout. For example, you may find one or several of the following general themes:

- justice
- honor
- honesty

- acceptance
- courage
- alienation
- duty
- responsibility
- freedom
- survival
- dignity
- self-respect
- passion
- loyalty

Also explore the broad ideas your story themes touch upon. This list might include the following:

- hurt that comes with loss
- loss of innocence
- the empowerment of women
- living life with a sense of humor
- the power of friendship
- overcoming all odds
- love conquers all
- good versus evil
- triumph over adversity
- man versus nature
- man versus himself

THE DEEPER THE MEANING,
THE MORE LASTING THE PROJECT

The two major plots—action and emotional—may convey different yet complementary thematic significance. Determining the thematic significance of both plots is the first step in creating the thematic significance that threads through your entire story. In chapter fourteen, you will learn how to convert these themes and meanings into an all-inclusive thematic significance statement. For the time being, we will focus on emotional and action thematic significance.

Emotional Thematic Significance

In F. Scott Fitzgerald's *The Great Gatsby*, Nick Carraway serves as the narrator. Of all the characters in the story, he is the only one who is changed by the action, thus making him the protagonist as well. (The protagonist is the character most changed by the dramatic action in the story. If more than one character is changed by the dramatic action, then the protagonist is determined by the degree and significance of the change.) Some might point to Gatsby, who is alive in the beginning and dead in the end, as the protagonist. But for the purposes of exploring thematic significance, we must focus not on the change from alive to dead but on how the dramatic action creates a long-term emotional change in a character.

Nick sets his emotional thematic significance in chapter three when he states that he is one of the few honest people he knows. Since he is the narrator, the reader is curious to know if he is reliable. Does Nick have a clear sense of himself from his time in the war, as he states? Or does he have more to learn about himself before he can accurately judge his honesty? In the end, Nick understands he has only begun to live up to the initial assessment of himself that he made in the beginning of the novel.

A thematic significance statement for Nick's character emotional plotline could be: "Only with maturity and by assuming personal and moral responsibility are we able to accurately judge other people and ourselves."

By the time you have completed a draft of your story, you have at least a vague idea of the deeper meaning of your story, what you are trying to say, and the ways you have attempted to communicate that meaning to your audience. As you continue evaluating the themes of your story, draft a rough statement that attempts to encompass the emotional thematic significance for the protagonist.

Action Thematic Significance

As is the case with all classic stories, *The Great Gatsby* deals with universal themes such as betrayal and love, loyalty and deception, family and violence, and life and death. Coupled with Nick's personal thematic significance statement is an overall thematic significance for the action of the story. A thematic significance statement for *The Great Gatsby* as a whole could be: "Ambition for money and another man's wife leads to destruction."

Just as you did for the emotional plot of your story, as you continue evaluating the themes of your story, draft a rough statement that attempts to encompass the action thematic significance. In other words, what do all of the scenes and action add up to mean in the end?

THEMATIC DETAILS

Every element in a memoir, novel, or screenplay contributes to the greater thematic significance of a story:

- Every character functions like a mirror reflecting back on the protagonist, revealing elements he can see in others but not in himself.
- Every subplot reflects the overall plot of the story.
- Every word contributes to the theme and mood and nuance.
- Just because the language is beautiful, the action clever, or the character quirky does not mean it belongs in the story. Every element must contribute to the deeper meaning of the piece.

To write a lasting and meaningful story, study carefully the themes you introduce in the beginning and develop in the middle. When the deeper meaning of your story reveals itself, it becomes a "eureka!" moment—that slap to your forehead when you understand what all the words in your story add up to mean.

Understanding the broad universal truths of your story, combined with the specific themes you choose, allows you to pinpoint the thematic significance of your piece. Characters snap to attention with a clear intent of their unique contribution to the overall story. Confusing subplots crystalize with meaning and symbolism. Random incidents become deliberate. Minor moments grow sublime. The challenge of making every word perfect becomes attainable.

SYMBOLS IN THE MIDDLE SCENES

There are two layers of meaning attached to every object: symbolic and literal. The symbolic layer carries the emotional meaning to the reader. The literal layer is the generally accepted or dictionary meaning for the object.

We introduced the idea of symbols in the last chapter. In the middle of the story, if the reader finds the same objects that were introduced in the beginning, she understands that these are not simple objects. Beyond the physical, measurable, and definable elements of an object, everything has a symbolic meaning attached to it.

Sometimes the meaning is universal. For instance, water can be symbolically viewed as the source of life: Creation myths from multiple cultures throughout history depict life emerging from water. Other times the meaning of a specific symbol is personal. For example, the circular nature of a ring has the universal meaning of the infinity and eternity, having no beginning and no end. Yet, to a specific character, a ring may be imbued with emotion—perhaps the ring was given as a gift from a loved one.

Symbolism connects your story to a deeper wisdom in each of us. Signs and symbols in scenes subtly guide the reader in the right direction toward the greatest understanding and impact.

You don't need to explain the main symbols, themes, and thematic details that were introduced or foreshadowed in the beginning and now appear throughout the middle of the story. They should simply appear along the story's path, whispering meaning and messages the reader needs to know. When used effectively (and not chosen randomly), symbols, words, metaphors, and dreams provide symbolic meaning, each one filled with a hidden message that contributes to the whole of the story. Some readers are better than others at interpreting signs, symbols, and messages contained in the smallest details.

Because the reader knows the characters more intimately in the middle through the action and conflicts the characters have reacted to and been broken by, she understands more deeply the symbols introduced in the beginning. The middle is the place to deepen the reader's understanding of the themes through figurative language and in the various forms you wish to use.

In *The Night Circus*, minor character Herr Friedrick Thiessen is hired to handcraft a clock—the Wunschtraum Clock—though he doesn't know its purpose until the middle. His is an extraordinary clock, but all clocks symbolize one thing over all else: the passage of time. Thiessen's clock is introduced on the first page of the novel: People "stare at the clock that sits just inside the gates that no one can properly describe."

Early in the middle of the novel, in a contemplative scene, Herr Thiessen learns that his elaborate, magical clock is meant for the circus of dreams. In this scene, Herr Theissen is vacationing in France. A friend mentions that a circus is in town and that the circus's clock is reminiscent of Thiessen's work. Curious, Thiessen, goes to the circus to see for himself.

We know this is a contemplative scene because Thiessen, a minor character, has a high rate of interior monologue (thought and rumination about the clock), and the scene moves at a slow pace to allow the reader to glean a deeper, more intimate look not into the protagonist's inner life but into the clock and circus's inner life.

> There is a considerable crowd outside when Herr Thiessen finally reaches the gates, and despite the crowd, he would have spotted his clock instantly, even without having been informed of its placement. It looms across from the ticket booth, just inside the large iron gates. It is about

to strike seven o'clock, and he stands back to watch it, letting the line for the tickets pass in front of him as the harlequin juggler pulls out a seventh ball from thin air, as the dragon's tale twitches and the clock chimes seven quiet chimes, barely audible over the din of the circus.

That the clock continues to appear throughout the middle of the novel informs the reader that the clock and the theme of time are thematically meaningful to this story. That the clock is fanciful and enchanting adds to the object's intrigue every time it reappears in the story.

By the recommitment scene at the end of the first half of the middle, which introduces the deeper middle, we are quite familiar with the ticking clock and all its wondrous features. Because we are repeatedly exposed to the clock and what it symbolizes, we find it even creepier and more worrisome when we learn that no one in or associated with the circus is aging.

The repetition of the clock in scenes throughout the middle of the story cements the theme of time, central to the circus and the story at large, in the mind of the reader. The symbolic colors of the clock—black and white—colors that traditionally represent the dichotomy of evil and good, night and day, further connect the reader to the story.

Archetypal Symbols

Archetypal symbols awaken an ancient wisdom in our collective unconsciousness from stories passed down through generations. The more unique and at the same time universal the symbol, the more often it can stir something deep in the reader.

The tiny antique oil painting of a goldfinch chained to a perch is a major archetypal symbol used in *The Goldfinch*. Birds are symbolic of freedom, as they have the ability to soar in the air without constraints. A goldfinch is predominately yellow and gold, which is the color of sunshine. The bird is associated with joy and energy that produces a warming effect in anyone who spots one. The chain around the goldfinch's leg, in contrast, symbolizes being bound and restrained. Thus, in this one small painting, three archetypal themes—freedom, joy, and restraint—juxtapose in such a way that they create a sense of unease, imbalance, and tension. They represent the desire to right a wrong, even if such a gesture is futile. In the same way, the characters in the story are shown as bound and chained by their beliefs, their positions in life, and their flaws.

The middle of *The Goldfinch* begins with an escape scene. Theo's father arrives to take him to Las Vegas, and the impending move comes just when Theo needs most to flee for his life. Getting away represents breaking free from his past pain and suffering. He also fears getting caught for stealing the tiny antique oil painting of the goldfinch, which is his last link to his mother and the girl who saved his life.

The push forward to Las Vegas also creates emotional duress and stress for him. Just before leaving with his father, Theo returns to the package room of the building where he had lived with his mother until her death. He has hidden the painting in this room. When a stranger blocks him from the suitcase that holds the painting, the sense of urgency creates unbearable tension. Anxious that Theo might not secure the painting and break free "in time," the reader is extremely nervous.

In this escape scene, the painting is barely mentioned. Instead, the doorman, Goldie, echoes the archetypal themes of the painting in his parting words to Theo. Goldie, too, is chained and unable to soar free in the warmth of the sun.

> "Have a good trip, amigo," he said—looking at me, then up at the sky. "Enjoy the sunshine out there for me. You know how I am about the sunshine—I'm a tropical bird, you know?"

The theme of escape is shown throughout the middle through Theo's drug and alcohol abuse and dangerous behavior. Just as the goldfinch in the painting is chained to his perch, Theo is confined and controlled by the past and his guilt. In addition to providing the central external conflict in this story and fertile ground for lots of dramatic action scenes, the painting continues to echo the theme.

WORD CHOICE

To create more drama and tension in the middle of a story, authors can carefully weigh one descriptive word over other evocative word choices. Striking upon the perfect descriptions deepens the reader's understanding of what the story means now that she has arrived in the middle. How the character responds and adjusts to the newness surrounding him in the unknown world of the middle further reinforces this understanding.

The words and objects and symbols in a suspense thriller are darker and edgier than word choices in a romantic comedy. The sentence structure in a chase scene is simpler and shorter and contains more dramatic verbs than a contemplative scene. Every object, sight, sound, odor, texture, and taste the protagonist experiences, surrounds himself with, and focuses on in the exotic world of the middle speaks to who he is emotionally, physically, and mentally. This knowing deepens the reader's appreciation of the story's thematic meaning.

Keep in mind that the energy and intensity of scenes build in the middle. The use of thematic details can provoke a greater degree of change.

When Theo moves to Las Vegas with his father and his father's girlfriend, the unbridled freedom he obtains—and the oppressive choices he continually makes—confine and numb him rather than bringing him liberation from his pain. Combined with the theme of freedom versus bondage is the theme of gambling. His father risks huge amounts of money in the hope of making lots more. Theo, too, gambles his life with his risky behavior. His desired result has nothing to do with money. He's hoping for relief from the tension of an unresolved past and an uncertain future, and from the massive responsibility of having stolen a world-class painting.

Theo meets Boris in Las Vegas, and they often hang out together, drinking and doing drugs.

> At the abandoned community center, the playground slides gleamed silver in the moonlight. We sat on the side of the empty fountain, our

> feet dangling in the dry basin, and passed the bottle back and forth
> until we began to lose track of time.

Setting the scene in an *abandoned* community center drives home the
point that neither Theo nor Boris has any sense of community other than
each other. For Theo to notice the *playground slide* while drinking until
he's dizzy reiterates the point of how far removed he is from a carefree
childhood. That the fountain is *empty* mirrors how truly empty Theo is.

Noun and Verb Choices

So far, you've been given examples of carefully considered nouns that
are used to reinforce the deeper meaning of a story: the goldfinch in the
stolen painting at the center of *The Goldfinch* and the handcrafted clock
in *The Night Circus*. Just as well-chosen nouns convey meaning, strong
active verbs can deepen and strengthen the chosen nouns.

That the goldfinch is "chained" to its perch in the valuable painting
helps define the deeper meaning of *The Goldfinch* than would an image
of the same bird in flight.

Any clock installed in the middle of the circus in *The Night Circus*
would have conveyed the importance of time in this story. The clock
the author describes doesn't simply tick time forward in a linear fash-
ion. Instead, the clock is magical, with a face that "shifts" from gray to
darker gray and then to black. (The colors gray and black symbolize and
reinforce the darker meaning of the story.) The body of the clock "turns"
itself inside out and "expands," helping to reinforce the story's focus on
both "real time" and the infinite nature of time. If the author had chosen a digital clock where the lighted image flashed forward to the next
minute in time, the reader would have gained an entirely different sense
of the story's meaning.

Cheryl Strayed, in her memoir *Wild*, uses a three-month hike alone
along 1,100 miles of the Pacific Crest Trail in California to explore the re-
demptive qualities of nature. In the middle of the memoir, she is barely
able to stand up with her backpack on her back, which speaks to the emo-

tional burden weighing her down. We would have perceived Cheryl's story much differently had she been able to carry the backpack with ease. Strayed states in the beginning of the middle her very specific goal for hiking the Pacific Crest Trail.

> I'd set out to hike the trail so that I could reflect upon my life, to think about everything that had broken me and make myself whole again.

The backpack represents the "everything" that broke her, and its heaviness makes her "falter" and "stagger," "moan" and "grumble" and need to "hunch" over in order manage her hefty load. In order to move, she has to practically "crawl." She "falters" and "dreads" going forward. These verbs differ from those used by a hiker she meets who had been "planning" his hike for years, "gathering" information, "corresponding" with hikers and "attending" long-trail hiking conferences. The second set of verbs help define the man who "rattles" off distances and elevations with ease.

The time you take to identify the perfect verb that will help reinforce the meaning of the noun and the story's overall thematic significance is well spent.

FORESHADOWING IN THE EMERGING MIDDLE

We'll discuss the darker aspects of foreshadowing in the next chapter. For our purposes in this chapter, think of foreshadowing as indicating in advance, portending, or giving an anticipatory sign or warning that something of great significance, often catastrophic or disastrous, is likely to happen in the future.

In the middle of *The Night Circus*, in a dialogue scene, the young circus-goer Bailey wanders into the fortune-teller's tent. The fortune-teller's "lovely elaborate sign" includes the words "Fates Foretold and Darkest Desires Disclosed." We know immediately that whatever Bailey learns in the tent will foreshadow what is to come later in the story for him, especially after we read this sentence: "The ongoing argument about his own future echoes in his ears as he enters the tent."

His early exchange with the fortune-teller gives us more specific information about this internal argument of his when she asks him what he would like to know.

> "About my future, " Bailey says. "My grandmother wants me to go to Harvard, but my father wants me to take over the farm."

Everything she says, and especially what she doesn't say, after his statement reveals what is coming in his plot, though in the early middle, the reader has no idea what her comments mean. Nor does Bailey. However, if you reread this scene after completing the entire novel, it is clear that all is revealed through foreshadowing. The scene points Bailey in a completely different direction than he had expected, which could classify it as both a dialogue scene and a twister scene.

In a contemplative scene from *Wild*, the author, while hiking alone:

> … came to a wide swath of snow on a steep incline, a giant ice-crusted sheath that obliterated the trail. It was like a rockslide, only scarier, a river of ice instead of stones. If I slipped while attempting to cross it, I would slide down the side of the mountain and crash into the boulders far below, or worse, fall farther into who knew what.

Though she successfully makes it across, "trembling but glad," she knows "that little jaunt was only a sample of what lay ahead." Thanks to this scene of foreshadowing, the reader knows it, too.

THEMATIC ELEMENTS ARE ALWAYS PRESENT

Even if you don't purposely broaden and deepen the themes and symbols introduced in the beginning and placed throughout the middle, they are still in your story, perhaps muddled and undeveloped and even confusing. The meanings of some symbols might not complement or contrast with the main themes. By completing the theme exercises in this section, you'll begin to grasp the important themes in your story. Writing middle scenes with the express purpose of working in the story's imagery, metaphors, mood, and tone, and bringing all of the elements together, makes for captivating, cohesive fiction.

In contrast to *The Goldfinch*, which explores themes and images of the lack of freedom and bondage, *Wild* uses the theme of travel to explore obtaining freedom.

Road trips generally symbolize movement and, often, the character's life journey. The middle of *Wild* is the wilderness trail trip. That she has no experience on the trail and only a guidebook (another symbol) for help effectively foreshadows all the chaos and challenges ahead. As the obstacles on the trail grow more perilous, her motivation and determination are challenged over and over again.

The Pacific Crest Trail becomes bumpier, riskier, and more perilous throughout the middle of the story, which is fraught with symbolic obstacles and setbacks such as losing one of her hiking boots, suffering blisters, snow, and frostbite, and encountering bears and the elements. The unexpected difficulties prove to be more demanding than she expected. They test her perseverance and require real effort and work just to survive the trail, much less achieve her goal of hiking to Oregon.

Other than evocative description of the setting around her, Strayed focuses most of her attention on her inner landscape, attempting to unravel what went wrong so she can heal and make her life better. During her internal rumination, she travels deeper and deeper into the wilderness, always putting one foot in front of the other and not always seeing much progress.

The unknown trail mirrors the trail to mental health and emotional wellness—a detail she doesn't recognize as she hikes. She is venturing forth in a new direction that requires survival skills. Every threatening element out in the wild parallels the threatening thoughts and feelings she deals with in her interior life. Each new obstacle in the middle becomes a symbolic gesture of overcoming fear and confronting intimidation.

Cheryl's feet are a powerful symbol throughout the memoir, as well as the hiking boots that cover her feet and carry her forward. The blisters, wounds, and snow-bitten flesh create mental and emotional sensory impressions and expand the reader's appreciation of the setting, mood, and character.

She becomes known on the trail as "... the famous Cheryl of the enormous backpack." As we discussed earlier, her backpack represents all the pain and sadness she lugs around with her everywhere, weighing her down. As much as the backpack signifies all her emotional baggage, it is often symbolic of the knowledge acquired over the years. In other words, though she is burdened by the past, what has come before also holds knowledge and wisdom vital to her well-being.

At the end of a transition scene near the halfway mark of the story, in which Cheryl travels by bus to avoid dangerous snowfall, she arrives at the station in Reno. "I fished three quarters out of my pocket," she writes, "played all three in the slot machine, and lost everything." The dialogue scene that follows takes place in the women's restroom, where a woman points to a feather Cheryl recently received from a fellow hiker she met on the trail.

> "It's got to be a corvid," she said, reaching over to touch it delicately with one finger. "It's either a raven or a crow, a symbol of the void," she added, in a mystical tone.
>
> "The void?" I'd asked, crestfallen.
>
> "It's a good thing," she said. "It's the place where things are *born*, where they *begin*."

When the image of losing money in the slot machine is presented along with the hopefulness of the feather, it lends insight and meaning to the reader about the difficulties Cheryl will likely encounter in her journey.

IN SUMMARY

- Imagery, symbols, metaphors, and settings introduced in the beginning are deepened and broadened in middle scenes.
- Symbols introduced earlier in the story may appear new in the exotic world of the middle.
- Repeating archetypal symbols reinforce and complement the small steps the character makes toward awareness and separation from her shadow.
- Word choices, and specifically noun and verb choices, help deepen and reinforce the overall story theme.
- Simple themes introduced in the beginning scenes are expanded in the middle scenes.

CHAPTER FOURTEEN

THEME IN THE DEEPER MIDDLE SCENES

A Darker Message and Meaning

Scene types addressed: recommitment scenes, twister scenes, dialogue scenes, love scenes, crisis scenes

Scenes in the deeper middle are fraught with tension as the protagonist approaches the Third Energetic Marker, Dark Night. Even in stories where the protagonist appears to be moving nearer to the successful completion of her goal, you will want to use imagery, symbols, and metaphors to foreshadow and warn the reader that all may not be as it appears. In this way, the scenes leading up to the Dark Night will keep the reader off balance, causing tension and thus ensuring that what occurs around three-quarters of the way into the story does not come as a complete surprise.

FORESHADOWING IN DEEPER MIDDLE SCENES

We've discussed the use of foreshadowing in chapter thirteen. Now, in the deeper middle, a more complete definition of foreshadow will prove helpful. The word *foreshadow*, when broken into two parts, defines itself.

Fore means situated or placed in front; it is a nonstandard form of *before*. In golf, it is the warning called out to people in the path of the ball. This golf term is relevant for our purposes because when you foreshadow in a story you are calling out a subtle warning to your reader about what's coming.

Shadow has two primary meanings. First, it is an area where light is obstructed by an object. Even more appropriate for our purposes here, and as defined in the introduction, is how shadow is defined in Jungian psychology: It is an aspect of a character's personality to which he is oblivious and includes everything outside the light of his consciousness, both positive and negative.

When you use foreshadowing, you are beforehand introducing a looming shadow within the character himself, in those close to him, and/or in the external action that will eventually define what comes later in the story.

Every word in a story moves readers in the direction the author wishes them to go, and foreshadowing is one means of pointing the way. John Green does this masterfully in *The Fault in Our Stars*. Around the midpoint of the story, at the Second Energetic Marker, is a twister scene demonstrating Augustus's rededication to his commitment. Hazel and her mother drive to his house to pick him up for their arranged flight to Amsterdam. As they approach his front door, they overhear someone crying inside the house, followed by Gus's all-in-caps declaration to his mother: "'BECAUSE IT IS MY LIFE, MOM. IT BELONGS TO ME.'"

In that moment, we understand that something is terribly wrong—our first hint of what is to come—even as, moments later, "the front door opened, and a smiling Augustus appeared, a roller bag behind him." All seems fine.

Later, in a dialogue scene in the deeper middle, as Hazel and Augustus enjoy supper along the canal in Amsterdam, Augustus explains the story behind the suit he is wearing.

> "… And I had my whole funeral planned out and everything, and then right before the surgery, I asked my parents if I could buy a suit, like a really nice suit, just in case I bit it. Anyway, I've never had occasion to wear it. Until tonight."
>
> "So it's your death suit."

To introduce that specific and purposeful word—*death*, the ever-present threat the two characters face daily—in the middle of a lovely dinner in a magical place shoves the shadow front and center between them and, in effect, creates a ticking clock.

The next scene opens after the meal, during dessert. Green could have chosen any delectable treat, yet he chooses one that foreshadows a delightful step forward in Hazel and Augustus's budding relationship.

> We were both really full, but dessert—a succulently rich *crémeux* sur-rounded by passion fruit—was too good not to at least nibble, so we lingered for a while over dessert, trying to get hungry again.

They aren't served just any fruit, mind you, but "passion fruit." The se-lection of the word *passion* foreshadows brilliantly what is coming when they return to the hotel and go up to his room.

USING THE FIVE SENSES

The warnings or foreshadowing that help to generate tension for the reader are often created through imagery that engages all five senses: sight, hearing, taste, smell, and touch. All big turning-point scenes, and especially those that fall in and around the Energetic Markers, benefit from the incorporation of all five senses. Descriptions rich in sensory detail bring more significance to these important scenes and transport the reader deeper into the middle of the story.

Taste

Of the primary taste sensations we perceive with our tongues, we have all experienced the following:

- bitter
- sweet
- sour
- salty
- savory

Taste evokes emotion and is a powerful and often underutilized sense in stories. Yet, when used successfully, taste pulls the reader into the story beyond what is seen and felt, and gives insight into what tastes good to the character and what turns her stomach.

When we finally arrive at the love scene in the deeper middle of *The Fault in Our Stars*, Hazel climbs on top of Augustus and takes off his shirt. She can "taste the sweat on the skin below his collarbone."

"Taste the sweat" evokes the readers' sense of taste and immediately pulls us into the intimacy of the moment. Augustus's sweating, paired with an earlier moment in which he winces in pain and loses his grip on the elevator door, subtly foreshadows that something is wrong with him.

Yet, before the reader can worry, Green immediately twists us away from Augustus's health as Hazel interprets his hesitancy as "trying to figure out a way not to hook up with me." She begins to blame herself for even suggesting the idea of going to his room in the first place.

Touch

The sense of touch is activated through our skin and feeds our brain information about the texture, temperature, pressure, and pain we encounter in our environment. In real life our skin is constantly coming in contact with the world around us, giving us immediate feedback. Aristotle attributed touch as the most universal of the senses because it is the most sensitive. Yet this sense is rarely used in stories.

In love scenes, physical contact, and thus the sense of touch, plays an essential role. Continuing with our earlier example, *The Fault in Our Stars*, after Augustus and Hazel shed their clothes in the hotel in Amsterdam and are lying on their backs next to each other, Hazel lets her hand trail down to the thickly scarred skin of Augustus's stump. He flinches and then denies that it hurts.

> He flipped himself onto his side and kissed me. "You're so hot," I said, my hand still on his leg.

Though Augustus continues kissing Hazel and she laughs at what he says, the reader either consciously or subconsciously registers the tactile detail of extreme heat, which creates an ever-growing tension of uncertainty about Augustus's health.

Hearing

The auditory system is the sensory center for hearing and the ability to detect and locate sounds in the environment and speech. Writers often rely heavily on the visual system of sight, describing what things, objects, places, and people look like and what characters see and recognize in each scene. Just as powerful is the sense of hearing. How well characters listen and attend to the auditory stimulation around them gives the reader insight into what is important to them and how sensitive they are to sound. It also helps create a story world that reflects the real world of the readers.

After Hazel and Augustus make love in *The Fault in Our Stars*, Augustus cannot keep his eyes open. Hazel surmises that this is the "one thing that followed type," yet the reader is left to wonder why he is suddenly so exhausted.

> His face turned away from me, my ear pressed to his chest, listening to his lungs settle into the rhythm of sleep.

The sound of his lungs settling stimulates the reader's sense of hearing. The reader hears what Hazel hears.

Later, in another twister scene, all of the foreshadowing is revealed in one awful moment when Augustus tells Hazel the truth: that his cancer has spread all over his body. He breaks down.

> … his sob roaring impotent like a clap of thunder unaccompanied by lightning, the terrible ferocity that amateurs in the field of suffering might mistake for weakness.

With Green's use of simile, likening his sobbing to thunder without lightning, he again activates the reader's auditory sense and more tightly ties the reader to the drama playing out between these two young people on the page.

Sight

Though Aristotle believed touch to be the universal sense, Plato vehemently disagreed, considering it the lowest sense. Instead, he held that the sense of sight was the highest sense, a system governed by "the soul's eye." Writers today seem content to hold true to his opinion by relying heavily on describing what characters see rather than touch and feel.

Our eyes give us information about the world around us and are used in almost every activity we undertake. Keep in mind that, although writers often cite the colors in a setting, the characters can also see the shape and movement and depth of what surrounds them.

Continuing with *The Fault in Our Stars*, after learning of Augustus's death sentence, Hazel reacts by crying.

> But even then he was strong, holding me tight so that I could see the sinewy muscles of his arms wrapped around me …

The reader, too, can see Augustus's strong arms with the help of the word choice *sinewy*, a visual image.

Green's use of sensory details in this twister scene allows the reader to experience moment by moment the same feelings and emotions that Hazel is experiencing and draws us intimately to her, until we feel as if we're actually her, the character in the scene.

Smell

Of the five senses, the olfactory sense, or sense of smell, is the most memorable and most closely tied to emotion. It is also the most difficult to convey. We have few words to describe the sense of smell beyond comparing one aroma to another familiar scent, which forces us to incorporate metaphor.

The earlier twister scene we described, where Augustus reveals that he is filled with cancer, could be considered a crisis scene, though it is not the true Dark Night of the Third Energetic Marker. Partly this is because this reveal is simply cognitive information that slams against the heart; he quickly follows the terrible news with his promise that "It'll be okay." This promise delays the massive reality from fully hitting Hazel and the readers, allowing them to briefly drop into denial.

However, at the darkest point in the deeper middle of the story, the full and tragic truth hits home in a full-blown crisis scene that we earlier described in this book. We know there is no turning back, no cure, nothing to fix or delay the horror.

Augustus calls Hazel for help in the middle of the night, and she finds him in his car in an empty parking lot outside a gas station. He is covered in his own vomit. She not only sees the tangible evidence of his ultimate downturn; she hears him moaning and smells his vomit, too.

> "Oh, God, Augustus, we have to get you to a hospital."
>
> "Please just look at it." I gagged from the smell but bent forward to inspect the place above his belly button where they'd surgically installed the tube. The skin of his abdomen was warm and bright red.

Hazel gags at the smell, turning his vomit real and sensory and experiential as the reader's sense of smell is provoked to remember exactly what vomit smells like. Additionally, in evoking that powerful smell, the reader's emotional memory of times of smelling vomit returns in full strength. In that same short paragraph, the reader also feels the warmth of his skin and sees how bright red and infected the area is.

Bringing in all the sensory details possible during the crisis at the Third Energetic Marker intentionally slows the pace and allows readers to not only read the words but also to become emotionally entangled in the scene by tapping into their physical senses.

There are moments in a story when all the senses gasp at once. These moments typically occur in scenes in and around the four Energetic Markers. The integration of all the senses in an impactful scene activates every sense in the reader for greater effect.

DARK AND EDGY THEMES

In the deeper middle, as antagonists become more challenging and the dark forces become more evil, and as the protagonist's flaw trips him up more often, writers frequently discover darker and edgier themes. It is common to shy way from the darker elements of your story. We often attempt to ignore or avoid the darkness and shadows, afraid we'll fall down and get hurt. Yet our fear is where the richest treasures lie.

As antagonists turn darker and edgier, the action they produce turns darker and edgier, too. The use of dark imagery, symbols, and metaphors creates uncertainty in the reader and lures her deeper into the story as she wonders what is amiss. Discover these deeper elements in your story to create more excitement in the action and elevate your story as a whole.

When you willingly risk embracing and integrating these darker and edgier themes, you become better able to imagine darker and edgier character goals that introduce a clearer emotional weight, and a more unique and compelling heart to your story, sending it to higher degrees of believability, originality, and mass appeal than the other books in its genre.

In chapter thirteen, you listed general themes in the beginning and middle of your story. Those themes often qualify as light themes, whereas in the deeper middle of your story, you may find that those same themes have turned darker. Here are some examples:

- Justice becomes Injustice.
- Honor turns to Dishonor.
- Honesty gives way to Dishonesty.

- Trust disintegrates into Distrust.
- Courage collapses into Cowardice.
- Responsibility crumbles into Irresponsibility.
- Confidence breaks down into Fear of Failure.
- Community converts into Isolation.
- Optimism degenerates into Negativity.
- Peace changes to Revenge.

Profound elements discovered in the deeper middle elevate your story concepts. Try switching the list of themes you generated in the earlier chapters from light to dark. Focus especially on those themes that are present in the beginning and continue all the way to the end. Examine your list, looking for meaning that feels true to your story.

THE THEMATIC SIGNIFICANCE STATEMENT

Plot is a series of scenes deliberately arranged by cause and effect to create dramatic action filled with conflict, tension, and suspense to further the character's emotional development and create thematic significance. Thematic significance ties your entire story together. It is the main thrust of your presentation and what you hope to prove through your story. The theme is the *why*: what you want your audience to take away after having read your story. The deeper meaning becomes the story's thematic significance.

After writing a couple of drafts and gaining a better understanding of what all the words in your story add up to, you can now reevaluate the broad ideas your story touches upon. Go through the list you generated in chapter thirteen, and, for each entry, tack on a qualifying phrase that shifts a common theme to a place of importance specific to your story.

The following italicized phrases have been pulled from the last chapter. In each case we have provided two opposite examples of possible outcomes to demonstrate how each theme can apply to two completely different stories.

Hurt that comes with loss …
> … is inevitable and brings about ultimate healing.
> … leads to revenge and destruction.

Loss of innocence …
> … leads to wisdom and a more mature happiness.
> … leads to cynicism and unhappiness.

The empowerment of women …
> … helps balance a world dominated by powerful men.
> … interferes with the status quo and leads to destruction.

Living life with a sense of humor …
> … helps offset disappointment and betrayal.
> … makes you seem foolish and simpleminded.

The power of friendship …
> … brings peace and understanding.
> … destroys the individual.

Overcoming all odds …
> … makes you strong.
> … makes you power hungry.

Try the exercise yourself by completing the following phrases:

- *Love conquers all …*
- *Good versus evil …*
- *Triumph over adversity …*
- *Man versus nature …*
- *Man versus himself …*
- *Crime doesn't pay …*
- *Believing in yourself …*
- *Accepting the differences of others …*

Now, attempt to combine the abstract ideas that seem the truest to your story with your story's observations about the human condition and what you are attempting to convey in your story specifically. Next, hone the statements into one sweeping thematic statement that incorporates all the major elements and feels like the truest and best representation of your entire story.

Whatever your thematic ideas, they need to be conveyed throughout the story and should reflect your beliefs about human nature or what you want to communicate about society at large. The sentence you generate about your story's deeper meaning reflects some element of life or human nature specific to your story. Ultimately your thematic significance statement emerges through observations of how your character changes over time because of the dramatic action, thus making the story meaningful.

A Tale of Two Cities is a beloved classic because of its promise of redemption and the possibility of transformation for both the individual and society. The thematic significance statement for this novel is: "A deeply flawed and wounded man brings meaning and value to his life and ascends to the level of hero in giving his life to save the lives of others." This statement embodies the action and the emotion plot while *the death of the old gives way to the new* applies to the political and action plots.

A Touchstone

Use the thematic significance statement as your touchstone and a continual reminder of the focus of your story. This statement should reflect the truth of your story. It doesn't have to be a universal truth or a truth for all time, but it does need to be true for *your* story. Use this statement to test the excellence of each scene in relationship to the whole. Often it is never directly stated but is implied through the actions and especially through the symbols, metaphors, and word choices that appear in the story.

As you rewrite and revise your story, you may find the need to reevaluate your thematic significance statement. For instance, if "digging deep and telling the truth" is needed for the protagonist to survive at the end and is included in your thematic significance statement, continually ask yourself if that is the case throughout the story. Is telling the truth important for your character, or does he need to learn a deeper lesson? Perhaps you find that your story doesn't reflect the idea of digging deep as much as letting go or taking the plunge.

Keep exploring your themes and abstract ideas in a similar way. What other themes do you find in your story? Do any of those belong in your statement? As you write, themes will emerge and you'll acknowledge and further incorporate them.

IN SUMMARY

You have a multitude of opportunities to help the reader emotionally connect at the sensory level to find meaning in your story. Foreshadowing is one occasion to do so. Using the five senses in turning-point scenes is another. The thematic significance statement for your story helps to define all the elements necessary in your individual story.

CHAPTER FIFTEEN

THEME IN THE END SCENES

Seams of Light

Scene types discussed: triumph scenes, resolution scenes, final scenes

Beneath the unfolding action and resulting emotion of your story, the reader collects each thematic fragment you've dropped along the way in the form of images, symbols, and character details, adding them up to form a mosaic of meaning. By the end of the story, if your reader can't follow this trail of crumbs and point to at least one theme, you probably have more work to do piecing it together. Either you don't know your themes yet (revisit chapter twelve for strategies on how to find your theme), or you have picked too minor a theme (you'll need to develop a more major one that will better encapsulate your entire story).

In the end scenes, now that your character has battled for her goals and overcome the antagonist(s), her reward will not only be literal or material—such as reuniting with her love or winning a prize—but also emotional and spiritual, in the form of her thematic transformation, i.e., the meaning she makes of her experience. Remember that symbols (objects and talismans) and images (poetically described images and metaphors), as well as word choice and sensory descriptions, allow you to point the reader directly to the theme without telegraphing it explicitly.

Look to who your character is at the beginning of your story to determine what thematic symbols you should pull in at the end scenes. Remember that characters are nearing integration by the end, coming into their full power and engaging in the final leg of their larger journey into the light of awareness. The end, the final quarter, comprises the Triumph as well as resolution and final scenes, all of which may take only a fraction of the pages of your novel, usually a quarter of the entire story.

SYMBOLS AND IMAGERY REFLECT CHARACTER INTEGRATION

In end scenes it is crucial to let your imagery reflect that your protagonist has undergone his integration into the light of his true, full, or new self. In Rene Denfeld's *The Enchanted,* The Lady begins the novel in a state of loneliness, which is reflected in the "dungeonlike stairs" and "dark corners" of the prison as she sees it. Her work, which requires her to be both compassionate and empathetic to the death-row inmates of the prison, exhausts her, and she labors to keep herself from the brink of an emotional breakdown, while questioning if this is the right work for her. By the end of the novel, The Lady seeks solace, as she always has, in nature, taking a drive to a place where the imagery becomes more hopeful.

> The sun caps each gentle wave. … She looks around and sees the blue forests rising up, like reassuring arms around her shoulders, embracing her as she wishes someone once embraced York and all the others.

The Lady understands now that all she needs to be responsible for is her own salvation, and there is still hope for that. And from the unlikeliest source, in the darkness of the ancient stone prison, she has found love and beauty in The Priest, who has sought to mend his own soul by tending to the spiritual fates of the death-row prisoners. The Lady and the Priest find in each other like-minded souls with troubled pasts. They have both been cast into the pit of a horrible place and have spent years redeeming themselves by helping those worse off. The imagery shifts to reflect that their time in the darkness is coming to an end.

In one scene, The Lady encounters The Priest, and Denfeld uses the symbol of his robes to point directly to the theme of finding one's authentic self.

> "Sometimes I imagine what you looked like in your robes," she suddenly says.
>
> He looks startled.
>
> "But I like you better this way," she continues. "I think I can see you now."

She sees him as he really is: not as the prisoners see him (the man who administers last rites), nor as he sees himself (a failure), but as a kind and loving man.

The Enchanted contains four powerful subthemes that are continually reinforced throughout the story: (1) finding beauty within horror; (2) making meaning in the most unlikely of situations and places; (3) redeeming one's past misbehaviors and crimes to flower into one's true, authentic self; and (4) seeing and accepting people as they really are, stripped of all their human foibles and flaws. The resonance of these themes at the end, when the only two characters not incarcerated face the possibility of a greater intimate connection, adds up to give the reader hope that both The Lady and The Priest can find the happiness they deserve.

And further toward the end, Denfeld gives us a taste of how that hope manifests between them. The reader is left with an image that shows The Lady and The Priest have, indeed, found a form of sustenance in each other.

> They are curled in a white bed under a steep eave, readying for sleep, and he is raising his face to watch her drift away. He is seeing her as if for the first time, how relaxed she looks, as if her entire body has found forgiveness from pain.

The "white bed under a steep eave" is an image of coziness and comfort that contrasts with the setting of the prison with its stone towers and crumbling walls, with its "loud slamming gates and shocking claps of metal locks." Denfeld repeats the theme of "seeing"—a product of compassion and understanding—and shows The Lady relaxed and in a state of forgiveness rather than loneliness, horror, or grief. It is clear at the end that The Lady has gained freedom, peace and rest, love and comfort. And The Priest's failures have not prevented him from finding love. The overarching theme that ties these subthemes together might be summed up as: "In the end, we are all human and deserving of love."

DEMONSTRATING THEME AT THE TRIUMPH

The Triumph, the high point for your protagonist and the point at which the antagonists are vanquished, is a moment of great thematic significance. If your character's plot has involved a "material" object, (such as the potent ring in *The Lord of the Rings*), a missing person, a lost treasure, or something else, then the physical thing or person may be the symbol you most need to emphasize at the Triumph. Many times, the protagonist will acquire this object at the Fourth Energetic Marker.

In Katherine Dunn's novel *Geek Love*, the "symbol" that carries the most powerful thematic resonance at the Triumph is a person. Oly Binewski, the albino dwarf, has a baby who was genetically created with the seed of her own brother, the megalomaniac Arty. (Fortunately the child is not conceived through incest, though the method of conception is no less horrifying.) Arty has spent the novel becoming a powerful cult leader, amassing throngs of cult followers, and terrorizing his circus family into obedience. Oly, by now, has realized that Arty's takeover of their circus will come to no good end, and all she wants is someone to love. She names her baby Miranda, for the pure and beautiful character in Shakespeare's play *The Tempest*, because "Miranda's father loved her."

Miranda is the only unsullied member of the Binewski family's circus freak show. She becomes symbolic now, representing love and strength: She is the best of both Oly and Arty, and mostly normal (other than a tail that is easily hidden). Miranda is the first person that Oly has ever loved more than the brother she has always idolized, more than the circus that she has called home. She narrates:

> Mama and I examined [Miranda's] amazing body and found only that ridiculous tail. My heart died. Arty would despise her.

And Arty does despise Miranda. He calls her a "norm" and deems her useless to their freak show. Oly knows her daughter is not safe, that if anyone good is to survive the culture of their bizarre world, she will have to send her baby away.

Oly's sweet and obedient younger brother Chick, who has a gift for moving things telekinetically and suppressing (or causing) pain with his mind, begins to turn against Arty when Miranda—the symbol of hope and goodness—is sent away. And when Arty causes the death of another key character with his arrogance, Chick's anger triggers his latent power, leading us to the Triumph. He blows up the entire circus, killing most of the characters in a lyrically described moment of light and fire.

> [Chick] turned away—and the fire came. The flames spouted from him—pale as light—bursting outward from his belly. … Arty and Al and Chick and the twins—gone dustward as the coals rid themselves of that terrible heat.

Oly, the sent-away baby Miranda, and Oly's now-demented mother Lil are the only survivors. But Dunn has planted the seed symbol of hope for a normal life in the form of Miranda, who has survived. Oly has lost everything, but at the same time she is free from the constraints of the freak show, free to discover who she really is. And Miranda is free to be who she will be rather than the person the shadows of the circus world would define.

CONTRAST BEGINNING THEMATIC ELEMENTS IN THE END SCENES

As we've said, you may not even begin to notice or plant the seeds of your theme until you've finished several drafts of your story. This is actually a good thing, as it allows you to consciously go back and weave in symbols and images throughout. Since your character has undergone a journey of transformation by your story's end, symbols are a lovely way to reflect that change in subtle ways.

The terms *shadow* and *light* we've discussed throughout this book are inordinately helpful when playing with your theme. If the beginning is the stage where you use your thematic elements to show that your character is deepest in the shadows, most unconscious and still bound by her wounds and history, then the end is the place where your thematic elements finally get to reflect the light of awareness, truth, honesty, and authenticity.

In *Dark Places* (even the title is thematically relevant), protagonist Libby Day, who has undergone an arduous journey to learn the truth about the murders of her mother and sisters, is no longer convinced that she has bad blood. The beginning scenes are peppered with dark, bleak imagery: "rotting ranch houses," her own innate "meanness," shirts with "mustardy armpits," and "drunk landlady eyes." These images reflect that she is depressed, hopeless, and self-loathing.

Contrast this with her final scenes, where she refers to the "curlicues of the prison barbed wire glowing yellow" and describes the trailer park as "pretty." There are "daffodils yellowing up everywhere" and "tulips." The color yellow, the beauty, the flowers all suggest hope and growth, things blooming (i.e., Libby herself growing) and coming into the light of truth, in sharp contrast to the shadow of dark secrets she had previously lived under.

And Flynn leaves us on an even higher note: Whereas Libby contemplates suicide in the beginning, at the end the author uses the following description of the setting to convey the hope in Libby's future.

No screams, no shotguns, no wild bluejay cries. Just listen to the quiet. … I just wanted to be some woman, heading back home to Over There That Way.

THEME IN THE RESOLUTION

Little story remains after the Triumph, though often a resolution scene (or scenes) unfolds, providing answers and tying up final threads left dangling. Here you may use a dialogue scene to reveal the final stage of your character's transformation or achievement of his goal, where two characters reflect in conversation about what has happened. Or you may plant the transformation in the narrative voice—in the internal monologue of a character as he reflects upon what meaning he has made of his journey.

In Julian Barnes's literary psychological thriller, *A Sense of an Ending*, the protagonist, Tony, has been left a legacy by an old schoolmate named Adrian, whose suicide was the engine that began the story. In the end scenes, Tony has finally come to understand his own selfishness, that he often put his own needs before others, which is revealed in dialogue with a therapist named Terry. The "Adrian" mentioned in the following dialogue is the grown but developmentally disabled son of the deceased elder Adrian. The fact that the young man shares his father's name, and that Tony feels somewhat responsible for the elder Adrian's death, evokes feelings in him.

> "Your presence upsets [Adrian]."
>
> "I'm sorry," I replied. "The last thing I want to do is upset him. I don't want to upset anyone any more. Ever."

This book does not end joyfully. Instead, the character at last understands his own actions, that he must atone for his faults, and that even youthful actions can have lasting effects. He may not be happy at the end, but he has matured. Barnes leaves us with some imagery that shows change.

> I thought of a cresting wave of water, lit by a moon, rushing past and vanishing upstream … .

It is amazing how often books end with images of light, be it sunlight or moonlight, the color yellow, or simply a seam of light through an open door or window. The subconscious is powerfully attuned to archetypal imagery, and light may be the most primal and simple representation of hope and change that exists.

At the end of Gillian Flynn's *Gone Girl*, we are brought full circle to the theme—"What is love?"—leaving us with a taste of what Amy has learned over the course of this wildly twisting novel. (For the record, Amy is something of an antihero, but her character still undergoes an arc of transformation.) In Amy's final internal monologue, she states:

> I was told love should be unconditional. That's the rule, everyone says so. But if love has no boundaries, no limits, no conditions, why should anyone try to do the right thing, ever?

Ending scenes do not have to be as subtle about theme as beginning scenes. Here you have the chance to drive home what the reader may have missed on a conscious level (but hopefully picked up on a subconscious level with your carefully dropped symbolic clues).

This doesn't mean you need be as pointed as Flynn, but you do have room in the end scenes to drive your theme home.

In *The Enchanted*, as the death row prisoner who narrates much of the book walks to the death chamber, he hears the following:

> In the distance, I hear the sweetest sound of all. It is a bird singing. Maybe it is one of the soft-tufted night birds, come to say goodbye. It is the most beautiful thing I have heard in many years, prettier than bells, and I know this trip was worth it just to hear that sound.

Keeping with the novel's theme of beauty found in horror, of the possibility of redemption even at the cusp of the end of life, this criminal who has done unspeakable things and is now facing his death hears the sweet sound of a bird singing goodbye. It's emotionally evocative, hitting the reader straight in the heart, begging us to consider that we are all human, all deserving of empathy at some point.

The end of *Geek Love* is a bit darker, though the image of hope remains in the form of Miranda, who was adopted as a toddler and is never subject to Arty's cruelty. Oly has kept watch on her daughter at a distance over the years, never revealing herself but making sure that Miranda is okay. When she has cause to believe Miranda is in danger—in the form of an antagonist known as Miss Lick, who intends to harm Miranda—Oly takes it upon herself to protect her daughter.

When Oly finally confronts Miss Lick, Dunn harks back to one of the other powerful themes of the novel: What is truly monstrous is rarely on the outside, like the twisted visages of the freaks of Oly's circus home, but rather inside people's corrupt hearts, leading them to do terrible things out of greed, lust, and power. Oly's brother Arty wasn't a monster because he looked like a lizard with flippers for arms, but because he wanted to be all-powerful and to enslave others to his will.

As Oly enacts her plan to save her daughter, the author chooses her words for Miss Lick carefully: "The monster is caught in the closet with her eyes stinging in the rising chlorine."

Miss Lick, who has made a business of disfiguring beautiful girls because she considers herself ugly, is monstrous on the inside, and Oly can't abide that kind of behavior any longer; she's lived her entire life in the shadow of it. Notably the scene is also enacted at an indoor swimming pool; if light is the universal symbol of hope and truth, then water is almost always an evocative symbol for emotion.

At the end of the novel, Oly makes the ultimate sacrifice for her child. Finding unconditional love is one of Oly's, and the novel's, many themes. Her daughter gives her that opportunity.

THEMATIC ELEMENTS IN THE FINAL SCENE

Ending scenes often come full circle, echoing and reflecting the beginning in a brighter, more hopeful, and integrated way.

The final scene is equally as important as the first scene but for an entirely different reason: Your reader will remember the thematic elements of your final scene for a long time, because it brings the whole journey to a close, while the first scene acts as a hook to draw the reader in but isn't always remembered this late in the game. Thus the images you use in this final scene are important; they linger and resonate long after the book is over.

We like to think of the final scene as providing a "snapshot" of where your protagonist is now. It doesn't have to tie everything up in a neat little bow—but it should convey symbolism of change, epiphany, or truth.

Here are a few images from final scenes we love. We are presenting them without context because we think it's clear what message they send, and you can probably extrapolate to figure out where the character started out.

- **FROM THE LITERARY NOVEL *PLAY IT AS IT LAYS* BY JOAN DIDION:** "I lie here in the sunlight, watch the hummingbird. This morning I threw the coins in the swimming pool, and they gleamed and turned in the water in such a way that I was almost moved to read them. I refrained."
- **FROM THE LITERARY THRILLER *IS THIS TOMORROW* BY CAROLINE LEAVITT:** "There was a shadow stretched out like an arm across the lawn, hurtling toward her. It struck her then, as if she were suddenly flooded with light. *Here we all are together.*"
- **FROM THE LITERARY NOVEL *SHINE, SHINE, SHINE* BY LYDIA NETZER:** "'Look,' said Sunny, and she pulled the scarf back to show the baby's face. 'She's here.'"
- **FROM THE APOCALYPTIC VAMPIRE NOVEL *THE PASSAGE* BY JUSTIN CRONIN:** "She felt it then: a rustling. Not heard but sensed, gliding atop every surface, every part of her, kissing it like a breeze. The skin of her hands and neck and face, the scalp under her hair, the tips of her eyelashes. A soft wind of longing, breathing her name."

USING PAIRED IMAGES

Another lovely way to bring your theme full circle is to pair a set of images in the beginning and end scenes, one in shadow, one in the light. For instance, you might show a bird at night in the beginning and show it again in daylight at the end. A rusted car can give way to a brand-new one. A locked door in the beginning can now be opened at the end.

One of our favorite sets of paired imagery comes from Gillian Flynn's thriller *Gone Girl*, a novel comprised of twister upon twister scenes that shift our understanding and loyalties to its two main characters through their alternating points of view, leaving the reader constantly unsure whom to believe.

The novel opens in Nick's point of view, describing an image of the first time he saw his wife, Amy.

> The very first time I saw her, it was the back of her head I saw, and there was something lovely about it, the angles of it. Like a shiny, hard corn kernel or a riverbed fossil. She had what the Victorians would call a finely shaped head.

At the beginning of the novel, even Nick doesn't realize just how much he doesn't know about his wife. Mentioning the back of her skull is a powerful way to symbolize his lack of understanding—it is a one-dimensional view of his wife—as well as to show that he was drawn to her when they first met for reasons that aren't based in logic or love, which ends up working against him.

At the end of the novel, after they have dragged each other through hell, Amy and Nick's true selves are revealed to each other, with severe consequences. In the final chapter in his point of view, he observes her skull once more.

> The other morning I woke up next to her, and I studied the back of her skull. I tried to read her thoughts. For once I didn't feel like I was staring into the sun.

At the end of his journey, Nick is wiser. He is no longer naïve about his, or his wife's, true nature, and without completely spoiling the ending, he is now matured into a kind of responsibility he didn't have at the beginning of his story. Flynn chooses the symbol of his wife's head to demonstrate that Nick finally understands the truth.

IN SUMMARY

- In the ending scenes, imagery reflects your character's procession into the light of integration to show hope, change, epiphany, and understanding, or simply the achievement of her goal.
- Contrast symbols from the beginning scenes, which show "shadow" thematic elements, with "light" elements in the end scenes to reflect your character's integration and change.
- Symbols can take the form of objects or people.
- Echo the theme from the beginning to the end through paired symbols.
- Thematic elements in the ending scenes do not have to be as subtle as in beginning scenes.

CONCLUSION

Throughout this book, we've pulled apart stories and scenes to demonstrate each of the three essential layers of story—action, emotion, and theme—separately. We've demonstrated especially how the layers serve to bring more impact to the major turning points of plot, the four Energetic Markers. We defined fifteen different scene types and then showed how the different scenes can be used to create more excitement, develop pacing, and convey emotion and meaning throughout the story.

We hope you will now understand where your strengths and weaknesses lie so you can move ahead, empowered by this new knowledge. For instance, you may have discovered that you are quite adept at writing action but need to focus on the powerful realm of emotion by paying attention to your character's internal reactions. Or you may find that you have a strong grasp of the Energetic Markers but now must learn how to use different types of scenes in between. Or you may get to the end and realize that your work lies in teasing out thematic threads, adding imagery, or honing your thematic significance statement, so the meaning of your story holds together with integrity.

Now that you understand the power that action, emotion, and theme serve in developing multifaceted scenes at the important turning points and throughout your entire story, it is time to weave the three layers together again. Remember that stories are built scene by scene, with all the plot threads intertwined and supporting each other.

If you are a writer who needs to establish the plot design first, start by identifying your Energetic Markers—they lay down the fundamental story and give you enough information about the trajectory of your character's journey to get started. Then walk through each phase of your story, asking some important questions as you make your way through each scene of the beginning, emerging middle, deeper middle, and end:

- Who is my character?
- How does she feel right here in this scene?
- What emotional stage of her journey is she at?
- What is her goal?
- How is/will the antagonist(s) oppose her?
- What does she need to do next?
- What will be the consequences?

If, conversely, you are a writer who has less trouble with the plot design and works best at the scene level, hopefully by now you've discovered how to use your chosen scene types to best effect. Maybe you have a tendency to rely heavily on action without giving much heed to emotion, or perhaps you currently have too many contemplative scenes that slow the pace. Now you'll want to draw from the palette of scene types we've provided and replace what isn't working.

If you get stuck on what scene comes next, consider where your character is in her emotional journey. If she's in the beginning, she won't be too confident or clear. If she's in the middle, life should get more complex for her, not easier. And if she's at the end, she should be more confident and certain than she was in earlier points in the story. Knowing your character's emotional plot helps you determine what action she needs to take next.

Or you may need to tighten up individual scenes or take them to new depths by tracking and fully integrating all aspects of plot, including these:

- **THE CHARACTER AND HER GOALS**
- **ANTAGONISTS AND ALLIES:** characters who thwart and support her goals
- **MOMENTUM:** also known as action, often in the form of dialogue and small motion, creating a sense of real time passing

- **NEW PLOT INFORMATION:** either a consequence of the last scene, or a new plot goal, so that each scene adds upon the last
- **SETTING AND TIME PERIOD:** revealed in sensory details and interactions, not summary
- **THEMATIC IMAGERY:** the overarching meaning of your story conveyed in image and sensory details throughout
- **TENSION:** a feeling of conflict and uncertainty that keeps the reader wanting and guessing

With this book as a guide you will now be able to recognize where you are top-heavy in one layer or underrepresented in another. You may see that your character's behavior in the middle fits better with the end and thus you may lay the groundwork for the new design of your story.

The better you are able to finesse your story by weaving together all of these elements in each scene, and especially at every Energetic Marker, the more alive your story will become for your reader and the more real your characters will feel. Well-written scenes allow the reader to enjoy the intellectual challenge presented in every story and, more important, to engage on an emotional level and viscerally take part in the character's journey.

We wish you deep writing!

Martha and Jordan

INDEX